MY FIRST SUMMER
IN THE
SIERRA

BY

JOHN MUIR

Edited and annotated by

Dr Laurence de B. Anderson

2018

(produced by Maricom Design)

Foreword.

John Muir was a man whose every cell thrilled to the ecstasy of the wild. This intensity of feeling is reflected in his writing – he really did want to make you feel everything he felt - up there in the mountain glory of the Sierra. The failure of words to convey precisely ever nuance of experience must have been frustrating – we are told that writing did not come easily to him, and that he re-worked his prose assiduously before publication.

As well as being a true lover of Nature, John Muir took a scientist's delight in classification and observation. Unfortunately, it is in these two-fold tendencies: the wordiness of the prose and his scientific delight in lists, that the modern reader may flounder. In addition, he was a Scots Presbyterian – and he used both religious and scientific ways of seeing the world. For these reasons I have taken the liberty of pruning some of the more enthusiastic sentences – while trying to keep his sense of freshness and keen observation alive. I have also annotated the work: clarifying religious or scientific references in square brackets [like this]. For the same reasons I have shortened the lists of species he encountered, and modified anachronistic spellings. True Muir aficionado's can return to the original if they wish!

However, I hope this homage to the great man's words meets with the approval of both Muir experts and the general public, who may gain a fresh understanding of one of the truly heroic and prescient Americans of the last two hundred years. In these days of environmental disaster, his words may inspire us to better care of our planet.

Dr Laurence de B. Anderson.

2018.

CHAPTER I

THROUGH THE FOOTHILLS WITH A FLOCK OF SHEEP. SUMMER, 1869.

Introduction.

In the great Central Valley of California there are only two seasons—spring and summer. The spring begins with the first rainstorm, which usually falls in November. In a few months the wonderful flowery vegetation is in full bloom, and by the end of May it is dead and dry and crisp, as if every plant had been roasted in an oven. Then the panting flocks are driven to the high, cool, green pastures of the Sierra.

I was longing for the mountains, but money was scarce and I couldn't see how I might get bread up there. Then Mr. Delaney, a sheep-owner, for whom I had worked before, offered to engage me to go with his shepherd and flock to the headwaters of the Merced and Tuolumne rivers: my intended area! I was in the mood to accept work of any kind that would take me into the mountains.

The flock, he explained, would be moved gradually up through the forest belts as the snow melted, stopping for a few weeks at the best places. These would be good centers of observation from which I could make many telling excursions. But I judged that I was in no way the right man for the place, and freely explained my shortcomings. Fortunately these seemed insignificant to Mr. Delaney. The main thing, he said, was to have a man he could trust to check on the shepherd, and assured me that any difficulties seemingly formidable at a distance would vanish as we went on; he encouraging me further by saying he would visit our camps to replenish our provisions. However, doubting myself, I feared that of the 2050 sheep, many would never return.

I was fortunate in getting a fine St. Bernard dog for a companion. His master, a hunter, came to me as soon as he heard that I was going to spend the summer in the Sierra and begged me to take Carlo with me, fearing that if he were compelled to stay all summer on the plains the fierce heat might be the death of him.

June 3, 1869. This morning provisions, camp-kettles, blankets, plant-press, etc, were packed on two horses, and we and the flock headed for the tawny foothills in a cloud of dust: Mr. Delaney, bony and tall, with hacked profile like Don Quixote, was leading the pack-horses; then Billy, the proud shepherd; a Chinaman; a Digger Indian to assist in driving for the first few days; and myself with notebook. The home ranch is south of the Tuolumne River near French Bar, where foothills of metamorphic gold-bearing slates dip below the stratified deposits of the Central Valley.

The flock traveled at the rate of about a mile an hour, outspread in the form of an irregular triangle. The old leaders showed by the eager, inquiring way they ran and looked ahead that they were thinking of the high pastures they had enjoyed last summer. Soon the whole flock seemed to be hopefully excited, the mothers calling their lambs, the lambs replying in tones wonderfully human, their fondly quavering calls interrupted now and then by hastily snatched mouthfuls of withered grass. The lambs and feeble old mothers dawdling in the rear were called the "tail end."

About noon the heat was hard to bear; the poor sheep panted pitifully and tried to stop in the shade of every tree they came to.

The trees, mostly the blue oak (*Quercus Douglasii*), are about thirty to forty feet high, with pale blue-green leaves and white bark, sparsely planted on the thinnest soil or in crevices of rocks beyond the reach of grass fires. The slates in many places rise abruptly through the tawny grass in sharp lichen-covered slabs like tombstones in deserted burying-grounds. Other than the oak (and some manzanita and ceanothus), the vegetation of the foothills is mostly that of the plains.

Now the scorching weather makes everything dreary. The ground is full of cracks, lizards gliding about on the rocks, and ants in amazing numbers, whose tiny sparks of life only burn the brighter with the heat. Magpies and crows, usually so noisy, are silent now, standing in mixed flocks on the ground beneath the best shade trees, with bills wide open and wings drooped, too breathless to speak; the quails also are trying to keep in the shade about the few tepid alkaline water-holes; cottontail rabbits are running from shade to shade among the ceanothus brush, and occasionally the long-eared hare is seen cantering gracefully across the wider openings.

After a short noon rest in a grove we carried on, climbing steadily till an hour before sunset, when we reached a dry ranch and camped for the night. The sheep were allowed to pick what they could find in the neighborhood until after sunset, watched by the shepherd while the others gathered wood, made a fire, cooked, unpacked and fed the horses, etc. About dusk the weary sheep were gathered on the highest open spot near camp, where they willingly bunched close together, and after each mother had found her lamb and suckled it, all lay down and required no attention until morning.

Supper was announced by the call, "Grub!" Each with a tin plate helped himself direct from the pots and pans while chatting about sheep-feed, mines, coyotes, bears, or adventures during the memorable gold rush days. The Indian kept in the background, saying never a word, as if he belonged to another species. The meal finished, the dogs were fed, the smokers smoked by the fire, and under the influences of fullness and tobacco an almost divine calm settled on their faces.

Then each with a sigh or a grunt knocked the ashes out of his pipe, yawned, gazed at the fire a few moments, said, "Well, I believe I'll turn in," and straightway vanished beneath his blankets. The fire flickered an hour or two longer, while in the starlight the flock looked like a big gray blanket.

June 4. The camp was astir at daybreak; coffee, bacon, and beans formed the breakfast, followed by quick dish-washing and packing. A general bleating began about sunrise.

We headed out after breakfast. Billy and the Indian and the Chinaman kept them moving along the weary road, and allowed them to pick up what little they could find. The starving flock had to be hurried on over the bare, hot hills to the nearest of the green pastures, about twenty or thirty miles from here.

The pack-animals were led by Don Quixote [Mr Delaney], a heavy rifle over his shoulder intended for bears and wolves. This day has been as hot and dusty as the first, leading over gently sloping brown hills, with mostly the same vegetation, excepting the strange-looking Sabine pine (*Pinus Sabiniana*), with its straggling branches and long gray needles, casting but little shade.

In general appearance this tree looks more like a palm than a pine. The cones are about six or seven inches long, about five in diameter, very heavy, and last long after they fall, so that the ground beneath the trees is covered with them. They make fine resiny, light-giving camp-fires, next to ears of Indian corn the most beautiful fuel I've ever seen. The nuts, the Don tells me, are gathered in large quantities by the Digger Indians for food.

June 5. This morning we gained the summit of the first well-defined bench on the mountain-flank at Pino Blanco, where there is a small field and vineyard irrigated by a stream that makes a pretty fall on its way down a little gorge.

After gaining the open summit of this first bench, feeling the natural exhilaration due to mild elevation of a thousand feet or so, and the hopes for the outlook, a magnificent section of the Merced Valley at Horseshoe Bend came in sight—a glorious wilderness that seemed to be calling with a thousand songful voices. Bold slopes feathered with pines and clumps of manzanita with sunny, open spaces between them, make up the foreground; the middle and background present fold beyond fold of finely modeled hills and ridges rising into low mountains.

The shaggy growth of chaparral looks like soft, rich plush without a single tree or bare spot. It extends, a heaving, swelling sea of green as regular and continuous as that produced by the Scottish heaths. The sculpture of the landscape is as striking in its main lines as in its lavish richness of detail; a grand congregation of massive heights with the river shining between, each carved into smooth, graceful folds without leaving a single rocky angle exposed.

I might have left everything for this whole landscape. Glad, endless work would then be mine: tracing the forces that have brought forth its features, its rocks and plants and animals and glorious weather! Beauty beyond thought everywhere, beneath, above, made and being made forever, so burned into mind and heart they surely can never grow dim.

The cool evening of this charmed day is cloudless and full of a kind of lightning I have never seen before—white, glowing, cloud-shaped masses down among the trees and bushes, like quick-throbbing fireflies in the Wisconsin meadows - rather than the so-called "wild fire." The spreading hairs of the horses' tails, and sparks from our blankets show how highly charged the air is.

June 6. Now on the second bench or plateau of the Range, and in open spots many of the lowland compositæ [Also called Asteraceae: nearly 33000 species; they are the daisies, essentially!] are still found, and some conspicuous members of the lily family; but the blue oak is left below, its place is taken by a fine large species (*Quercus Californica*) with deeply lobed deciduous leaves, picturesquely divided trunk, and broad, massy, finely lobed and modeled head.

At about twenty-five hundred feet we come to the edge of the great coniferous forest, made up mostly of yellow pine with just a few sugar pines. We are now in the mountains proper and they in us, kindling enthusiasm, making every nerve quiver, filling every pore and cell of us. Our flesh-and-bone tabernacle [biblical reference to the human body] seems transparent as glass to the beauty about us, as if an inseparable part of it, thrilling with the air and trees, streams and rocks, thrilling in the waves of the sun—a part of all Nature, neither old nor young, sick nor well, but immortal.

Just now I can hardly conceive of any bodily condition dependent on food or breath any more than the ground or the sky. How glorious a conversion, so complete and wholesome it is, scarce memory enough of old bondage days left as a standpoint to view it from!

In this newness of life we seem to have been so always.

Through openings in the pine woods I see snowy peaks about the headwaters of the Merced above Yosemite. How near they seem and how clear their outlines in the blue air - as far as I can I must drift about these love-monument mountains, glad to be a servant of servants in so holy a wilderness.

Found a lovely lily (*Calochortus albus*) in a shady adenostoma thicket near Coulterville, in company with *Adiantum Chilense*. It is white with a faint purplish tinge inside at the base of the petals, a most impressive plant, pure as a snow crystal, one of the plant saints that all must love.

The yellow pine cones are held upside down on the ground by the Douglas squirrel, and turned around gradually until stripped, while he sits usually with his back to a tree, probably for safety. Strange to say, he never seems to get himself smeared with gum.

We are now approaching the region of clouds and cool streams.
Magnificent white cumuli appeared about noon above the Yosemite
region - floating fountains refreshing the glorious wilderness—sky
mountains in whose pearly hills and dales the streams take their rise.
No rock landscape is more varied in sculpture, none more delicately
modeled than these landscapes of the sky; domes and peaks rising,
swelling, white as finest marble and firmly outlined, a most
impressive manifestation. Every rain-cloud leaves its mark; on the
rocks are its marks engraved whether we can see them or not.

I have been examining the curious and influential shrub *Adenostoma
fasciculate,* forming a dense, almost impenetrable growth that looks
dark in the distance. It belongs to the rose family and grows on sun-
beaten slopes. Like grass is often swept away by running fires, but is

quickly renewed from the roots. Any trees that may have established themselves in its midst are at length killed by these fires, and this no doubt is the secret of the unbroken character of its broad belts. A few manzanitas, which also rise again from the root after consuming fires, dwell with it, also a few bush compositæ—baccharis and linosyris, and some liliaceous plants, mostly calochortus and brodiæa, with deepset bulbs safe from fire. A multitude of birds and "wee, sleekit, cow'rin', tim'rous beasties" [from Robbie Burns's famous poem "To a Mouse"] find good homes in its deepest thickets, and the open portions fringing the margins of its main belts offer hospitality to the deer when winter storms drive them down from their high pastures. A most admirable plant! It is now in bloom, and I like to wear its pretty fragrant racemes in my buttonhole.

Azalea occidentalis, another charming shrub, grows beside cool streams here and much higher in the Yosemite. We found it in bloom a few miles above Greeley's Mill, where we are camped. It is related to the rhododendrons, very showy and fragrant, and everybody must like it not only for itself but for the shady alders and willows, ferny meadows, and living water associated with it. Another conifer was met with today: incense cedar (*Libocedrus decurrens*), a large tree with warm yellow-green foliage in flat plumes like those of arborvitæ, bark cinnamon-colored. The limbless boles of the old trees make striking pillars in the woods, worthy companions of the kingly sugar and yellow pines. I feel strangely attracted to this tree - its fragrant, brown close-grained wood, the small scale-like leaves, and the flat overlapping plumes (which make fine beds and shed the rain). It would be delightful to be storm-bound beneath one of these noble old trees, its broad sheltering arms bent down like a tent, incense rising from the fire made from its dry fallen branches, and a hearty wind chanting overhead. But the weather is calm tonight, in our mere sheep camp.

We are near the North Fork of the Merced. The night wind is telling the wonders of the upper mountains, their snow fountains and gardens, forests and groves; even their topography is in its tones.

And the stars, the everlasting sky lilies, how bright they are now that we are above the lowland dust! The horizon is bounded and adorned by a spiry wall of pines, every tree harmoniously related to every other; definite symbols, divine hieroglyphics written with sunbeams. Would I could understand them! The stream flowing through ferns and lilies makes sweet music, but the pines marshaled around the edge of the sky make a yet sweeter music to the eye. Divine beauty all. Here I could stay tethered forever with just bread and water, nor would I be lonely; loved friends and neighbors would seem all the nearer however many the miles and mountains between us.

June 7. The sheep were sick last night, having been eating azalea. The California sheep owner is in haste to get rich, and often does, now that pasturage costs nothing, while the climate is so favorable that no winter food supply, shelter-pens, or barns are required. Therefore large flocks may be kept at slight expense, and large profits realized, the money invested doubling, it is claimed, every other year. This quickly acquired wealth usually creates desire for more. Then indeed the wool is drawn close down over the poor fellow's eyes, dimming or shutting out almost everything worth seeing.

As for the shepherd, his case is still worse, especially in winter when he lives alone in a cabin. He is solitary most of the year, and solitude to most people seems hard to bear. He seldom has much good mental work or recreation. After his dull drag all day after the sheep, he must get his supper. Perhaps no bread is baked; he just makes a few grimy flapjacks in his unwashed frying-pan, boils a handful of tea, and perhaps fries a few strips of rusty bacon, then depends on the genial stupefaction of tobacco for the rest - to bed, often without removing the clothing. He finally becomes semi-insane or wholly so.

The shepherd in Scotland, on the other hand, is probably descended from a race of shepherds and inherited a love and aptitude for the business almost as marked as that of his collie. He sees his family and neighbors, has time for reading in fine weather, and often carries books to the fields. The oriental shepherd, we read, called his sheep by name, but the California shepherd, as far as I've seen or heard, is never quite sane for any considerable time.

The sick sheep are getting well, and the shepherd is discoursing on the various poisons lurking in these high pastures—azalea, kalmia, alkali. After crossing the North Fork of the Merced we made a considerable ascent on a rocky, brush-covered ridge to Brown's Flat, where for the first time since leaving the plains the flock is enjoying plenty of green grass.

Before noon we passed Bower Cave, a delightful marble palace, not dark and dripping, but filled with sunshine, which pours into it through its wide-open mouth facing the south. It has a fine, deep, clear little lake with mossy banks embowered with broad-leaved maples, all under ground, wholly unlike anything I have ever seen. It is claimed by a Frenchman, who has fenced and locked it, placed a boat on the lakelet and seats on the mossy bank under the maple trees, and charges a dollar admission fee.

Poison oak or poison ivy (*Rhus diversiloba*), is somewhat troublesome to most travelers, inflaming the skin and eyes, but blends harmoniously with its companion plants. I have oftentimes found the curious twining lily (*Stropholirion Californicum*) climbing its branches. Sheep eat it without apparent ill effects; so do horses. Like most other things not apparently useful to man, it has few friends, and the blind question, "Why was it made?" goes on and on with never a guess that first of all it might have been made for itself.

Brown's Flat is a shallow fertile valley on the top of the divide between the North Fork of the Merced and Bull Creek, commanding magnificent views in every direction. Here the adventurous pioneer David Brown made his headquarters for many years, dividing his time between gold-hunting and bear-hunting. It was as a bear-hunter that Brown became famous. His hunting method, as described by Mr. Delaney, who had passed many a night with him and learned his stories, was simply to go slowly and silently through the best bear pastures, with his dog and rifle and a few pounds of flour, until he found a fresh track and then follow it to the death, paying no heed to the time required. When high open points were reached, the likeliest places were carefully scanned. The time of year enabled the hunter to determine approximately where the bear would be found—in the spring and early summer on open spots about the banks of streams and springy places eating grass and clover and lupines, or in dry meadows feasting on strawberries; toward the end of summer, on dry ridges, feasting on manzanita berries. In late autumn, when acorns are ripe, Bruin's favorite feeding-grounds are groves of the California oak in park-like canyon flats. ['Bruin' is a generic name for 'bear'].

"Whenever," said the hunter, "I saw a bear before it saw me I had no trouble in killing it. I studied the lay of the land and got to leeward no matter how far around I had to go, and then worked up to within a few hundred yards or so, at the foot of a tree that I could easily climb, but too small for the bear to climb. Then I looked well to the condition of my rifle, took off my boots so as to climb well if necessary, and waited until the bear turned its side in clear view when I could make a sure or at least a good shot. In case it showed fight I climbed out of reach. Oh yes, bear-hunting is safe enough when followed in a safe way, though like every other business it has its accidents, and little doggie and I have had some close calls.

Bears like to keep out of the way of men as a general thing, but if an old, lean, hungry mother with cubs met a man on her own ground she would, in my opinion, try to catch and eat him. This would be only fair play anyhow, for we eat them, but nobody hereabout has been used for bear grub that I know of."

Brown had left his mountain home before we arrived, but a considerable number of Digger Indians still linger in their cedar-bark huts on the edge of the flat. They were attracted in the first place by the white hunter whom they had learned to respect, and to whom they looked for guidance and protection against their enemies the Paiutes, who sometimes made raids across from the east side of the Range to plunder the stores of the comparatively feeble Diggers, and to steal their wives.

CHAPTER II

IN CAMP ON THE NORTH FORK OF THE MERCED

June 8, 1869. The sheep, now grassy and good-natured, nibbled their way down into the valley of the North Fork of the Merced at the foot of Pilot Peak Ridge to the place selected by the Don for our first central camp, a picturesque hollow formed by converging slopes at a bend of the river. Here we made racks in the shade of the river-bank trees, and beds of fern fronds, cedar plumes, and various flowers, each to the taste of its owner, and a corral back on the open flat for the sheep.

June 9. How deep our sleep last night in the mountain's heart, beneath trees and stars, hushed by solemn waterfalls and many small voices whispering peace! And our first pure mountain day, warm, calm, cloudless—how immeasurable it seems, how serenely wild! Along the river, over the hills, in the ground, in the sky, the work of spring goes on with joyful enthusiasm, new life, new beauty, unfolding, new birds in their nests, new winged creatures in the air, and new leaves, new flowers, rejoicing everywhere.

The close trees about the camp give ample shade for ferns and lilies, while back from the bank the sunny spots call up the grasses and flowers in glorious array, tall bromus waving like bamboos, starry compositæ, [list of other species] gilias, violets, glad children of light. Soon every fern frond will be unrolled, great beds of common pteris and [several species names] on sunny rocks. Some of the woodwardia fronds are already six feet high.

A handsome little shrub, *Chamæbatia foliolosa*, belonging to the rose family, spreads a yellow-green mantle beneath the sugar pines for miles without a break, not mixed with other plants, except the occasional Washington lily nodding above its even surface, or a bunch of tall bromus. This fine carpet shrub begins to appear at, say, twenty-five hundred feet, is up to knee high, has brown branches, and the largest stems are only about half an inch diameter. [Description of the species]. Am delighted with this little bush. It is the only true carpet shrub of this part of the Sierra. The manzanita, rhamnus, and most of the species of ceanothus make shaggy rugs and fringes rather than carpets.

The sheep do not take kindly to their new pasture, perhaps from being too hemmed in by the hills. They are never fully at rest. Last night they were frightened, probably by bears or coyotes prowling for a grand mass of mutton.

June 10. Very warm. We get water from a rock basin at the foot of a picturesque cascading reach of river. The rock here comprises black knobs of metamorphic slate, worn smooth and contrasting with the cascading water falling in lace-like sheets and braided currents. Tufts of sedge growing on the rock knobs just above the surface produce a charming effect, the long elastic leaves arching, the tips of the longest in the current, to see how beautiful a happy stream can be made. The giant saxifrage also grows on some of the knobs, displaying their broad, round, umbrella-like leaves in showy groups. The flowers of this species (*Saxifraga peltata*) are purple, and form tall racemes that bloom before the appearance of leaves. The fleshy root-stocks grips in cracks and hollows, enabling the plant to hold on against floods—a species employed by Nature to make yet more beautiful these cool clear streams. The trees arch from bank to bank, making a leafy tunnel full of subdued light, through which the young river sings a happy living creature.

Heard a few peals of thunder from the upper Sierra, and saw firm white clouds rising back of the pines. This was about noon.

June 11. On one of the eastern branches of the river discovered some charming cascades, each ending in a pool. White dashing water, a few tufts of carex leaning over with fine effect, and large orange lilies in groups on fertile soil-beds.

There are no large meadows or plains near camp to supply lasting pasture for our thousands of nibblers. Their main dependence is ceanothus brush on the hills and tufted grass patches here and there, with lupines and pea-vines among the flowers on open spaces. Large areas have already been stripped bare or nearly so, compelling our woolly bundles to scatter far and wide, keeping the shepherds and dogs very busy. Mr. Delaney has gone back to the plains, taking the Indian and Chinaman with him, leaving instructions to keep the flock here or hereabouts until his proximate return.

How fine the weather is! Nothing more celestial can I conceive. Scarce can these tranquil air-currents be called winds - the very breath of Nature, whispering peace to every living thing. Down in the dell no swaying of tree-tops; most of the time not a leaf moves. I've not seen a single lily swinging on its stalk, though they are so tall the least breeze would rock them. What grand bells they have! Some of them big enough for children's bonnets. I have been sketching them, and would fain draw every leaf, every curved and spotted petal. Better kept gardens cannot be imagined. The species is *Lilium pardalinum,* five to six feet high, leaf-whorls a foot wide, flowers about six inches wide, bright orange, purple spotted in the throat—a majestic plant.

June 12. A slight sprinkle of rain—large drops far apart, falling with hearty plash on leaves and stones and into the mouths of the flowers. Cumuli rising to the eastward. How beautiful their pearly bosses! Mountains of the sky - never before have I seen clouds so substantial in form and texture. Nearly every day toward noon they mushroom up as if new worlds were being created. Hovering fondly over the gardens and forests with their cooling shadows and showers, they keep every petal and leaf in glad heart. One may fancy the clouds themselves are plants, springing up at the call of the sun, growing in beauty until they reach their prime, scattering rain and hail like berries and seeds, then wilting and dying.

The mountain live oak, common here and a thousand feet or so higher, is like the live oak of Florida, not only in general appearance, foliage, bark, and wide-branching habit, but in its tough, knotty wood. Standing alone with plenty of elbow room, the largest trees are about seven to eight feet in diameter near the ground, sixty feet high, and as wide or wider across the head. [Description of the species].

A marked plant is the bush poppy (*Dendromecon rigidum*), found on the hot hillsides near camp, the only woody member of the order I ever met. Its flowers are light orange, an inch to two wide, fruit-pods three or four inches long, slender and curving, the bush height about four feet, made of many slim, straight branches - a companion of the manzanita and other sun-loving chaparral shrubs.

June 13. Another glorious Sierra day in which one seems to be dissolved and absorbed and sent pulsing onward we know not where. Life seems neither long nor short, and we take no more heed to save time or make haste than do the trees and stars. This is true freedom, a good practical sort of immortality. Yonder rises another white skyland. How sharply the yellow pine spires and the palm-like crowns of the sugar pines are outlined on its smooth white domes. And hark! the grand thunder billows booming, rolling from ridge to ridge, followed by the faithful shower.

A good many herbaceous plants come this far up the mountains from the plains, and are now in flower, two months later than their lowland relatives. Saw a few columbines today. Most of the ferns are in their prime: rock ferns on the sunny hillsides, cheilanthes, [list of species] and the common *Pteris aquilina* on sandy flats. This last makes shows of abounding beauty to set the botanist wild with admiration. I measured some at more than seven feet high. The broad-shouldered fronds held high on smooth stout stalks growing closely and overlapping, make a complete ceiling, beneath which one may walk erect over several acres, as if beneath a roof. How lovely the light streaming through this living ceiling, revealing a framework of countless panes of pale green and yellow plant-glass nicely fitted together—a fairyland created out of the commonest fern-stuff.

The smaller animals wander about as if in a tropical forest. I saw the entire flock of sheep vanish at one side of a patch and reappear a hundred yards farther on at the other, their progress betrayed only by the jerking and trembling of the fronds; though strangely, very few of the woody stalks were broken. Sitting, I never enjoyed anything in the way of a bower of wild leaves more strangely impressive. Only spread a fern frond over a man's head and freedom and beauty and peace come in, displacing mundane cares. The waving of a pine tree on the top of a mountain—a magic wand in Nature's hand, but the beauty value of what the Scotch call a breckan [group of ferns] in a still dell, what poet has sung this? No-one, however encrusted with care, could escape the Godful influence of these sacred fern forests.

Yet this very day I saw a shepherd pass through one of the finest of them without betraying more feeling than his sheep. "What do you think of these grand ferns?" I asked. "Oh, they're only damned big brakes," he replied. ['Brake' implying a dense stand of low vegetation to be struggled through].

Lizards of every style dwell here, seemingly as happy as the birds and squirrels. Lowly, gentle fellow mortals, enjoying God's sunshine, and doing their best to get a living. I like to watch them at their work and play. One loves them the better the longer one looks into their beautiful, innocent eyes. As they dart about on the hot rocks, swift as dragonflies, the eye can hardly follow them. They only run about ten or twelve feet, then stop, going all their journeys by quick, jerking impulses. They are short-winded, and when pursued steadily they are soon breathless and easily caught. Their bodies are more than half tail; these seem to follow the body lightly enough.

Some are colored like the sky, bright as bluebirds, others gray like the lichened rocks on which they hunt and bask. Even the horned toad of the plains is a mild, harmless creature, and so are the snake-like lizard species which glide in curves with true snake motion, dragging their small, useless limbs. I watched one specimen fourteen inches long make no use whatever of its tender, sprouting limbs, but glided with all the sly grace of a snake.

Now running about my feet is a little, gray, dusty fellow who seems to trust me, looking up into my face. Carlo makes a quick pounce, for the fun of the thing I suppose; but Liz has shot away like an arrow, and is safe in the recesses of chaparral. Gentle saurians, dragons, descendants of an ancient and mighty race, Heaven bless you and make your virtues known! for few of us know as yet that scales may cover fellow creatures as gentle and lovable as those with feathers, or hair, or cloth.

Mastodons and elephants [mammoths] used to live here no great time ago, as shown by their bones discovered by surface gold miners. Bears of at least two species are here now, besides the California mountain lion, and wild cats, wolves, foxes, snakes, scorpions, wasps, tarantulas; but one is tempted to regard a savage black ant as the master existence of this vast mountain world. These fearless imps, though only about a quarter of an inch long, are fonder biting than any beast I know, attacking every living thing around their homes. Their bodies are mostly jaws curved like ice-hooks, and to employ these weapons seems to be their chief pleasure. Most of their colonies are established in living oaks somewhat decayed or hollowed, probably because of their strength in repulsing the attacks of animals and storms. They work both day and night, creep into dark caves, climb the highest trees, hunt through cool ravines and hot ridges, and extend their highways over everything but water and sky.

From the foothills to a mile above sea level nothing can stir without their knowledge; and alarms are spread in an incredibly short time, without any cry that we can hear [alarm is spread by release into the air of pheromones]. There seems to be no common sense in their ferocious courage (beyond the defense of home) - they fight anywhere and always. Though torn limb from limb, they will yet hold on and die biting deeper. When I contemplate this fierce creature so widely distributed and strongly entrenched, I see that much remains to be done ere the world is brought under the rule of universal peace and love.

On my way to camp a few minutes ago, I passed a dead pine nearly ten feet in diameter. It has been burnt and now looks like a grand black pillar set up as a monument. A colony of large jet-black ants have established themselves, laboriously cutting tunnels and cells through the shaft. The entire trunk seems to have been honeycombed, judging by the gnawed chips like sawdust piled up around its base. They are more intelligent looking than their smaller, strong-scented brethren, and have better manners. Their towns are carved in fallen trunks as well as standing, but never in sound, living trees or under ground.

When you sit down or take notes near a colony, some wandering hunter is sure to find you and come cautiously forward to investigate. If you are not too near the town and keep perfectly still he may run across your feet a few times, over your legs and hands and face, up your trousers, as if taking your measure and getting comprehensive views, then go in peace without raising an alarm. If, however, a tempting spot is offered or some suspicious movement excites him, a bite follows, and such a bite! I fancy that a bear or wolf bite is not to be compared with it. A quick electric flash of pain along the outraged nerves, and you discover how great is your capacity for sensation! A shriek, a grab for the animal, and a bewildered stare follow this bite of bites as one comes back to consciousness from the sudden eclipse. With care, one need not be bitten oftener than once or twice in a lifetime.

This wonderful, electric species is about three fourths of an inch long. Bears are fond of them, and tear their home-logs to pieces, roughly devouring the eggs, larvæ, parent ants, and the rotten or sound wood of the cells, all in one spicy acid hash. The Digger Indians also are fond of the larvæ and even of the adult, so I have been told. They bite off the head, and eat the tickly acid body. Thus are the poor biters bit, like every other biter in the world's great family.

There is also a fine, active, intelligent-looking red species, intermediate in size between the above. They dwell underground, and build large piles of seed husks, leaves, straw, etc., over their nests. Their food is insects and plant leaves, seeds and sap. How many mouths Nature has to fill, how many neighbors we have, how little we know about them, and how seldom we get in each other's way! Think of the infinite numbers of even smaller fellow mortals, compared with which the smallest ants are as mastodons.

June 14. The basins below the falls and cascades are kept nicely clear of detritus. The heavier material swept over the falls is heaped in front of the basins like a dam, thus tending to increase their size. However, during the spring floods, when the snow is melting and the upper tributaries are roaring loud from "bank to brae," [Scots Gaelic: brae = hill], then boulders which ordinary currents are unable to move are swept forward as if by a mighty besom [broom], over the falls, and pile up in a new dam, together with part of the old one. Some of the smaller boulders are carried further downstream and variously lodged according to size and shape. But the greatest

changes made in these relations of fall, pool and dam are caused, not by the ordinary spring floods, but by extraordinary ones. The testimony of trees growing on flood boulder deposits shows that a century or more has passed since the last master flood came to awaken everything movable to go swirling and dancing. These floods may occur during summer storms called "cloud-bursts." They fall on wide, steeply inclined stream basins furrowed by converging channels, which suddenly gather the waters together into the main trunk in booming torrents of enormous transporting power, though short-lived.

One of these ancient flood boulders stands firm in the middle of the stream channel near our camp. It is a nearly cubical mass of granite about eight feet high, plushed with mosses to ordinary high-water mark. When I climbed on top of it today and lay down to rest, it seemed the most romantic spot ever—the one big stone with its mossy level top like an altar, the fall bathing it in the finest of spray, the clear green pool beneath, with its foam-bells and half circle of lilies, and flowering trees leaning over all in sun-sifted arches. Beneath that leafy, translucent ceiling, how delightful the water music: bass tones of the fall, the ringing spray, and infinite variety of small low tones of the current. All this shut in; every one of these influences acting as if in a quiet room. One might hope to see God.

When the camp was sleeping I groped my way back to the altar boulder and lay there all night - above the water, beneath the leaves and stars—everything still more impressive than by day. Precious night, precious day to abide in me forever! Thanks be to God for this immortal gift.

June 15. Another reviving morning. Down the long slopes the sunbeams gild the awakening pines, cheering every needle, filling every living thing with joy. Robins are singing in the alder and maple groves, the same old song that has sweetened countless seasons over most of our blessed continent. In this hollow they are as at home as in farmers' orchards. Bullock's oriole and the Louisiana tanager are here also, with many warblers and other little mountain troubadours, most now busy about their nests.

Discovered another magnificent specimen of the goldcup oak, six feet in diameter, a Douglas spruce seven feet, and a twining lily (*Stropholirion*), with stem eight feet long, and sixty rose-colored flowers.

Found a sugar pine cone today nearly twenty-four inches long and six in diameter, the scales being open. Another specimen nineteen inches long; the average length of full-grown cones on trees favorably situated is nearly eighteen inches. At about twenty-five hundred feet they are smaller, a foot to fifteen inches long, and at seven thousand feet (near its limit) about the same size. This noble tree is an inexhaustible source of pleasure: its grand tassel cones, its perfectly round bole one hundred feet or more without a limb, the purplish bark, and its magnificent feathery arms forming a striking crown. It looks somewhat like a palm, but no palm displays such majesty of form and behavior either when poised silent and thoughtful in sunshine, or wide-awake waving in storm winds with every needle quivering. When young it is very straight, like most other conifers; but at the age of fifty to a hundred it begins to acquire individuality, so that no two become alike. Every tree calls for special admiration; I regret that I cannot draw every needle.

It is said to reach a height of three hundred feet, though the tallest I have measured is around 240 feet. The diameter of the largest near the ground is about ten feet, though I've heard of some twelve feet thick or even fifteen. The diameter is held to a great height, the taper being almost imperceptibly gradual.

Its companion, the Yellow Pine, is almost as large. The silvery foliage of the young specimens forms cylindrical brushes on top shoots and the ends of branches, and when the wind sways the needles all one way the tree becomes a tower of quivering sun-fire. Well may this shining species be called the silver pine. The needles are sometimes more than a foot long, almost as long as those of the long-leaf pine of Florida. Were there no sugar pine, then would this be the king of the world's eighty or ninety species, the brightest of the multitude [there are about 630 species of pines!]. Were they mere mechanical sculptures, what noble objects they would still be! And how many other radiant resiny sun trees are here and higher up—libocedrus, Douglas spruce, silver fir, sequoia. How rich our inheritance in these blessed mountains.

June 16. One of the Indians from Brown's Flat got right into the middle of the camp this morning. I was seated on a stone, looking over my notes and sketches, and was startled to see him standing grim and silent within a few steps of me, as motionless and weather-stained as an old tree-stump. All Indians seem to have learned this wonderful way of walking unseen, making themselves invisible like certain spiders which, in case of alarm, immediately bounce themselves up and down on their elastic threads so rapidly that only a blur is visible. The wild Indian power of escaping observation, even where there is little or no cover to hide in, was probably slowly acquired in hard lessons while trying to approach game, take enemies by surprise, or get safely away. And this experience transmitted through many generations seems at length to have become what is vaguely called instinct. [A sort of Lamarckian idea].

How smooth is the surface of the mountains about us! Trackless except on small open spots on the sides of the streams, or where the forest carpets are thin. On these open strips and patches deer tracks may be seen, and the great suggestive footprints of bears.

Along the main ridges and larger branches of the river, Indian trails may be traced, but they are not nearly as distinct as one would expect to find them. How many centuries Indians have roamed these woods nobody knows, probably a great many, extending far beyond the time that Columbus touched our shores, and it seems strange that heavier marks have not been made. Indians walk softly and hurt the landscape hardly more than the birds and squirrels, and their brush and bark huts last hardly longer than those of wood rats, while their more enduring monuments, excepting those wrought on the forests by the fires they made to improve their hunting grounds, vanish in a few centuries.

How different are most of those of the white man, especially on the lower gold region—roads blasted from rock, streams tamed and forced out of their channels along the sides of canyons and valleys to work in mines like slaves. Crossing high in the air between ridges on long straddling trestles as if flowing on stilts, or across valleys and hills imprisoned in iron pipes to wash away hills and the skin of the mountain's face, stripping every gully and flat. These are the white man's marks made in a few feverish years, to say nothing of mills, fields, villages, scattered all along the Range. Long will it be ere [before] these marks are effaced, though Nature is doing what she can, replanting, sweeping away old dams, leveling gravel piles, patiently trying to heal every scar. The main gold storm is over, except a few gray old miners scratching a living in waste diggings.

Thundering underground blasting is still going on to feed the pounding mills, but their influence on the landscape is light as compared with the pick-and-shovel storms of a few years ago. Fortunately for Sierra scenery, the gold-bearing slates are mostly in the foothills. The region about our camp is still wild, and higher lies the snow, trackless as the sky.

Only a few hills and domes of cloudland were built yesterday and none at all today. The light is peculiarly white and thin, though pleasantly warm. The serenity of mountain weather in spring, just when Nature's pulses beat highest, is one of its greatest charms. There is only a moderate breeze from the summits at night, and a slight breathing from the sea and the lowlands during the day, or stillness so complete no leaf stirs. The trees hereabouts have but little wind history to tell.

Sheep, like people, are ungovernable when hungry. Excepting my guarded lily gardens, almost every leaf that these hoofed locusts can reach within a mile or two of camp has been devoured. Even the bushes are bare. In spite of dogs and shepherds the sheep scatter to all points of the compass and vanish in dust. I fear some are lost, for one of the sixteen black ones is missing.

June 17. Counted the wool bundles this morning as they bounced through the narrow corral gate. About three hundred are missing, and as the shepherd could not go to seek them, I had to. I tied a crust of bread to my belt, and set out with Carlo for the upper slopes of the Pilot Peak Ridge. I had a good day, notwithstanding the care of seeking the silly runaways. I went out for wool, and did not come back shorn. A peculiar light circled the horizon, white and thin like that of the auroral corona, blending into the blue of the upper sky.

The only clouds were a few faint flossy pencilings like combed silk. I pushed direct to the boundary of the usual range of the flock, and around it until I found the outgoing trail of the wanderers. It led far up the ridge into an open place surrounded by a hedge of chaparral. Carlo knew what I was about, and eagerly followed the scent until we came to them, huddled in a silent bunch. They had been there all night and all the forenoon, afraid to go out to feed. Having escaped restraint, they were, like some people, afraid of their freedom, did not know what to do with it, and seemed glad to get back into the old familiar bondage.

June 18. Another inspiring morning, nothing better in any world can be conceived. No description of Heaven that I have ever heard seems half so fine. At noon the clouds occupied about .05 of the sky [about one twentieth], white filmy touches drawn delicately on the azure.

The high ridges and hilltops beyond the woolly locusts are now gay with monardella, clarkia, coreopsis, and tall tufted grasses, some of them tall enough to wave like pines. The lupines, of which there are many ill-defined species, are now mostly out of flower, and many of the compositæ are beginning to fade, their radiant corollas vanishing in fluffy pappus like stars in mist.

We had another visitor from Brown's Flat today, an old Indian woman with a basket on her back. Like our first caller from the village, she got fairly into camp and was standing in plain view. How long she had been quietly looking on, I cannot say. Even the dogs failed to notice her stealthy approach. She was on her way, I suppose, to some wild garden, probably for lupine and starchy saxifrage leaves and rootstocks. Her dress was calico rags, far from clean. She seemed sadly unlike Nature's neat well-dressed animals, though living like them on the bounty of the wilderness. Strange that mankind alone is dirty. Had she been clad in fur, or cloth woven of grass or shreddy bark, like the juniper and libocedrus mats, she might then have seemed a rightful part of the wilderness; like a good wolf or bear. But from no point of view are such debased fellow beings a whit more natural than the tourists that frighten the birds and squirrels.

June 19. Pure sunshine all day. How beautiful a rock is made by leaf shadows! Those of the live oak are particularly clear, beyond all art in grace and delicacy, now still as if painted on stone, now gliding softly as if afraid of noise, now waltzing in swift, merry swirls, or jumping on and off in quick dashes like wave embroidery on seashore cliffs. How true is this shadow beauty, and with what sublime extravagance is beauty thus multiplied! The big orange lilies are now arrayed in all their glory of leaf and flower. Noble plants, in perfect health, Nature's darlings.

June 20. Some of the silly sheep got caught fast in a tangle of chaparral this morning, like flies in a spider's web, and had to be helped out. Carlo found them and tried to drive them from the trap by the easiest way. How far above sheep are intelligent dogs! No helper can be more constant than Carlo. The noble St. Bernard is an honor to his race.

The air is distinctly fragrant with balsam and resin and mint, every breath of it a gift we may thank God for. Who could ever guess that so rough a wilderness should yet be so full of good things? One seems to be in a majestic domed pavilion in which a grand play is being acted with scenery and music and incense - all the furniture and action so interesting we are in no danger of boredom. God seems to be always doing his best here, working in a glow of enthusiasm.

June 21. Sauntered along the riverbank to my lily gardens. The perfection of beauty in these lilies is a never-ending source of admiration and wonder. Their rhizomes are set in black mould accumulated in hollows of the metamorphic slates beside the pools, where they are well watered without being subjected to flood action. Every leaf in the level whorls around the tall polished stalks is as finely finished as the petals, and the light and heat required are measured for them and tempered in passing through the branches of over-leaning trees. However strong the winds from the noon rainstorms, they are securely sheltered. Beautiful hypnum carpets bordered with ferns are spread beneath them, violets too, and a few daisies. Everything around them sweet and fresh like themselves.

Cloudland today is only a solitary white mountain; but it is so enriched with sunshine and shade, the tones of color on its big domed head and bossy outbulging ridges, and in the depressions between them, as to be ineffably fine.

June 22. Unusually cloudy. Besides the periodical shower-bearing cumuli there is a thin, diffused, fog-like cloud overhead. About .75 in all [about ¾ of the sky covered in cloud].

June 23. Oh, these vast, measureless mountain days, inciting one at once to work and rest! Days in whose light everything seems equally divine, opening a thousand windows to show us God. One who gains the blessings of one mountain day might nevermore faint by the way, no matter how tired; whatever his fate, he is rich forever.

June 24. Our regular allowance of clouds and thunder. Shepherd Billy is bothered about the sheep; he declares they are possessed with more of the evil one than any other flock from the beginning of the invention of mutton and wool. No matter how many are missing, he will not, he says, go a step to seek them, because while getting back one he would probably lose ten. Therefore runaway hunting must be Carlo's and mine. Billy's little dog Jack is also giving trouble by leaving camp nightly to go visit up the mountain at Brown's Flat. He is a common-looking cur, but tremendously enterprising in love and war. He has cut all the ropes he has been tied with, until his desperate, after climbing the brushy mountain again and again to drag him back, fastened him [by various means] but he escaped as usual and reached the Indian settlement in safety. His master followed, and gave him a beating, and swore that next evening he would "fix that infatuated pup" by anchoring him unmercifully to the heavy cast-iron lid of our Dutch oven.

Before morning, however, Jack was heard far up the height howling Excelsior ["Excelsior" implies doing something to the utmost], cast-iron anchor notwithstanding. Next night, dog, pot-lid and all were tied up in an old bean-sack, and thus at last angry Billy gained the victory. Just before leaving home, Jack was bitten in the lower jaw by a rattlesnake, and his whole head region was swollen to more than double the normal size; nevertheless he was after a week completely recovered. The only treatment he got was gallons of fresh milk forcibly poured down his sore, poisoned throat.

June 25. Though only a sheep camp, this grand mountain hollow is home, every day growing sweeter, and I shall be sorry to leave it. The lily gardens are safe as yet from the trampling flock. Poor, dusty, hungry creatures, I pity them. Many a mile they must go daily to gather their fifteen or twenty tons of chaparral and grass.

June 26. Nuttall's flowering dogwood makes a fine show when in snowy white bloom. The involucres are six to eight inches wide. Along the streams it is thirty to fifty feet high, with a broad head when not crowded. It attracts a crowd of moths, butterflies, and other winged people about it for their own and the tree's advantage. It likes cool water, and drinks like the alder, willow, and cottonwood, flourishing best on stream banks, though often found in damp shady glens beneath the pines, where it is smaller. When the leaves ripen in fall, they are mor beautiful than the flowers, in tones of red, purple, and lavender. Another abundant chaparral shrub on the shady sides of the hills, is [probably] *Cornus sessilis*. The leaves are eaten by the sheep. Heard a few lightning strokes in the distance, with mumbling reverberations.

June 27. The beaked hazel (*Corylus rostrata*, var. *Californica*) is common on cool slopes up Pilot Peak Ridge. There is something peculiarly attractive in the hazel, an attraction inherited from our forefathers. This species is four or five feet high, leaves soft and hairy, grateful to the touch, and the delicious nuts are eagerly gathered by Indians and squirrels. The sky as usual adorned with white noon clouds.

June 28. Warm, mellow summer. The glowing sunbeams make every nerve tingle. The new needles of the pines and firs are nearly full grown and shine gloriously. Lizards are glinting about on the hot rocks; some that live near the camp are more than half tame. They seem attentive to our every movement, as if curious to simply look on, turning their heads to look back, and making pretty gestures. Gentle, guileless creatures with beautiful eyes, I shall be sorry to leave.

June 29. There is a very interesting little bird that flits about the waterways of the river. It is not a water-bird in structure, though it gets its living in the water, and never leaves the streams [the American *dipper* (Cinclus mexicanus)]. It is not web-footed, yet it dives fearlessly into deep swirling rapids, evidently to feed at the bottom, using its wings to swim with under water as loons do. In shallow places, it thrusts its head under in a jerking, nodding way that attracts the attention. About robin sized, it has short wings serviceable for flying either in water or air, and an upslanted tail of moderate size, giving it a wrennish look. Its color is bluish ash, with a brown tinge on head and shoulders. It flies from with a solid whir of wing-beats like those of a quail. Usually alighting on a rock in the stream, it can perch on dry limb of an overhanging tree. It has the oddest, mincing manners imaginable; and the little fellow can sing too, a sweet, thrushy song.

What a romantic life this bird leads on the most beautiful portions of the streams. No wonder it is a fine singer, considering the stream songs it hears. Every breath the little poet draws is part of a song, for all the air about the river is beaten into music, and its first lessons must begin by the thrilling and quivering of the eggs in unison with the tones of the falls.

June 30. Half cloudy, half sunny, clouds lustrous white. The tall pines crowded along the top of the Pilot Peak Ridge look like six-inch miniatures exquisitely outlined on the satiny sky. Average cloudiness for the day about .25. No rain. And so this memorable month ends, a stream of beauty unmeasured, no more to be sectioned off by almanac arithmetic than sun-radiance or the currents - a peaceful, joyful stream of beauty. Every morning, arising from the death of sleep, the happy plants and animals seemed to be shouting, "Awake, awake, rejoice, rejoice, come love us and join in our song. Come! Come!" Looking back through the romantic, enchanting peace of the camp grove, this June seems the greatest of all the months of my life. Everything in it seems equally immortal and

divine—one smooth, pure glow of Heaven's love, never to be blotted by anything past or to come.

July 1. Summer is ripe. Flocks of seeds are already out of their cups seeking their predestined places. Some will strike root beside their parents, others flying on the wings of the wind, alighting among strangers. Most of the young birds are feathered and out of their nests, though still looked after, fed and to some extent being educated. How beautiful the home life of birds! No wonder we all love them.

I like to watch the squirrels. There are two species here, the large California gray and the Douglas.

The latter is the brightest of all the squirrels I have ever seen, making every tree tingle with his prickly toes, a condensed nugget of fresh mountain vigor and valor, as free from disease as a sunbeam. One cannot think of such an animal ever being weary or sick. He seems to think the mountains belong to him, and at first tried to drive away the whole flock as well as shepherd and dogs. How he scolds, and what faces he makes, all eyes, teeth, and whiskers! If not so comically small, he would indeed be a dreadful fellow. I should like to know more about his life in the home knot-hole and tree-tops throughout all seasons. Strange that I have not yet found a nest. The Douglas is closely allied to the red squirrel of the Atlantic slope, and may have come to this side of the continent by the great unbroken forests of the north.

The California gray is one of the most beautiful, and, next to the Douglas, the most interesting of our hairy neighbors. Compared with the Douglas he is twice as large, but far less lively as a worker in the woods and he manages to make his way with less stir than his small brother. I have never heard him bark at anything except our dogs. He glides silently from branch to branch, examining last year's cones, to see whether some few seeds may not be left, or gleans fallen ones among the leaves on the ground, since none of the present season's crop is yet available. His tail floats now behind him, above him, level, or gracefully, every hair in place, shining and radiant as thistle-down in spite of gummy work. His whole body seems about as unsubstantial as his tail. The little Douglas is full of brag and fight, with movements so quick they almost sting the onlooker, and the gyrating show he makes turns one giddy to see. The gray is shy, and stealthy, as if half expecting an enemy in every tree and bush, manifesting no desire to be seen. The Indians hunt them for food, a good cause for caution, not to mention hawks, snakes and wild cats.

Where food is abundant they wear paths through thickets and over prostrate trees to some favorite pool where they drink at nearly the same hour every day. These pools are closely watched, especially by the boys who lie in ambush with bow and arrow. In spite of enemies, squirrels are happy fellows; of all Nature's wild beasts, they seem to me the wildest. May we come to know each other better.

The chaparral slope to the south of the camp is the hiding-place of the curious wood rat or pack rat (*Neotoma*), a handsome, interesting animal. It is more like a squirrel than a rat [description]. No rat or squirrel has so innocent a look, or expresses such confidence. He seems too fine for the thorny thickets he inhabits. No other animal inhabitant of these mountains builds houses so large and striking in appearance. The traveler will not be likely to forget them: built of all kinds of sticks, old rotten pieces, green prickly twigs bitten from the nearest bushes, the whole mixed with miscellaneous odds and ends, such as clods, bones, deerhorn, etc., piled up in a conical mass as if it were got ready for burning. Some of these curious cabins are six feet high and as wide at the base. A dozen or more of them are occasionally grouped together, possibly for sharing food and shelter.

The solitary explorer happening into one of these strange villages may fancy himself in an uncanny Indian settlement. But no savage face will he see, perhaps not a single inhabitant, or at most two or three seated on top of their wigwams, looking at the stranger with the mildest of eyes, and allowing a near approach.

In the centre of the spiky hut a nest is made of the inner fibres of chewed bark, and lined with feathers and the seed down such as willow and milkweed. Some of these soft nests are built in trees forty feet from the ground, and even in garrets, as if seeking the company and protection of man, like swallows. Among housekeepers Neotoma is considered a thief, because he carries away everything transportable to his queer hut: knives, forks, combs, nails, tin cups, spectacles, and so on—merely, however, to strengthen his fortifications, I guess. His food at home is nearly the same as that of the squirrels—nuts, berries, seeds, and sometimes the bark and tender shoots of the various species of ceanothus.

July 2. Sunny day, thrilling plant and animals and rocks alike, making sap and blood flow fast, and making every particle of the crystal mountains swirl and dance in glad accord like star-dust. No dullness anywhere, no stagnation, no death. Everything kept in joyful rhythmic motion in the pulses of Nature's big heart.

Pearly cumuli over the higher mountains, no silver lining, but all silver. The brightest, rockiest-looking clouds, most varied in features and keenest in outline I ever saw. The daily building of these snowy cloud-ranges—the highest of Sierra's—is a prime marvel to me.

But in the midst of these mountain affairs a change of diet is pulling us down. We have had no bread a few days, and miss it unreasonably, for we have plenty of meat and sugar and tea. Strange! The Indians put us to shame, so do the squirrels—starchy roots and seeds and bark in abundance, yet the failure of the meal sack disturbs us and threatens our best enjoyments.

July 3. Warm. Breeze just enough to sift through the woods and waft fragrance from their thousand fountains. The pine cones are growing well, balsam dripping from every tree, and seeds are ripening fast, promising a fine harvest. The squirrels will have bread. They eat all kinds of nuts long before they are ripe, and yet never seem to suffer in stomach.

CHAPTER III

A BREAD FAMINE.

July 4, 1869. The air beyond the flock range, is growing sweeter and more fragrant with woodland perfumes from day to day. Mr. Delaney is expected to arrive soon with new provisions. In the meantime our stock of beans as well as flour has failed—everything but mutton, sugar, and tea. The shepherd is somewhat demoralized. He says that since the boss has failed to feed him he is not rightly bound to feed the sheep, and swears that no decent white man can climb these steep mountains on mutton alone. "It's not fittin' grub for a white man. For dogs and coyotes and Indians it's different. Good grub, good sheep. That's what I say." Such was Billy's Fourth of July oration.

July 5. The noon clouds on the high Sierra seem yet more indescribably beautiful from day to day as one becomes[Pg 76] more aware of them. The smoke gunpowder burned yesterday on the lowlands, and the eloquence of the orators has blown away by this time. Here every day is a holiday, a jubilee ever sounding with serene enthusiasm, without weariness. Not a single cell or crystal unvisited or forgotten.

July 6. Mr. Delaney has not arrived, and the bread famine is sore. We must eat mutton a while longer, though it's hard to get used to it. I have heard of Texas pioneers living without bread for months without suffering, using the breast-meat of wild turkeys for bread.

Of this kind they had plenty in the good old days when life was more risky but less fussed over. The trappers of early Rocky Mountain days regions lived on bison and beaver for months. Salmon-eaters among both Indians and whites seem to suffer little from the want of bread.

We pick out the leanest bits of mutton, and down they go, causing nausea and an effort to reject the offensive stuff. Tea makes matters worse. The stomach begins to assert itself as an independent creature. We should boil lupine leaves, clover, petioles, and saxifrage roots like the Indians. We try to ignore our gastric troubles, rise and gaze about us, turn our eyes to the mountains, and climb doggedly up into the heart of the scenery. A stifled calm comes on, and the day's duties and even enjoyments are languidly got through with. We chew ceanothus by way of lunch, and smell the spicy monardella for the head and stomach-ache that now lightens, now comes muffling down upon us and into us like fog. At night more mutton, flesh to flesh, down with it, not too much, and there are the stars shining through the cedar plumes above our beds.

July 7. Rather sickish this morning, and all about a piece of bread. Can scarce command attention to my best studies, as if one couldn't take a few days' saunter in the Godful woods without maintaining a base on a wheat-field and gristmill. Like caged parrots we want a cracker. Bread without flesh is a good diet, as on many botanical excursions I have proved. Tea also may easily be ignored. Just bread and water and delightful toil is all I need—not unreasonably much, yet one ought to be trained to full independence of any particular kind of nourishment. That this may be accomplished is manifest in the lives of people of other climes. The Eskimo, for example, gets a living far north of the wheat line, from oily seals and whales, yet these people of the frozen shores of our continent are said to be hearty, jolly, stout, and brave. We hear, too, of fish-eaters, carnivorous as spiders, yet well enough as far as stomachs are concerned, while we make wry faces over our fare, looking sheepish in digestive distress amid rumbling, grumbling sounds that might well pass for smothered baa's. We have a large supply of sugar, and this evening I thought these belligerent stomachs might possibly, like complaining children, be coaxed with candy. Accordingly a lot of sugar was cooked to a sort of wax, but this stuff only made matters worse.

Man seems to be the only animal whose food soils him, making necessary much washing and napkins. Moles eating slimy worms are as clean as seals or fishes, whose lives are one perpetual wash. And the squirrels in these resiny woods keep themselves clean in some mysterious way; not a hair is sticky, though they handle the gummy cones, and glide about apparently without care. Birds, too, are clean, though they seem to make a good deal of fuss cleaning their feathers. Certain flies and ants I see are in a fix, entangled and sealed up in the sugar-wax we threw away, like some of their ancestors in amber. Our stomachs are sore with long squirming.

Once I was very hungry in the Bonaventure graveyard near Savannah, Georgia, having fasted for several days; then the empty stomach seemed to chafe and pain in much the same way as now. We dream of bread, a sure sign we need it. Like the Indians, we ought to know how to get the starch out of fern and saxifrage stalks, lily bulbs, pine bark, etc. Our education has been sadly neglected for many generations. Wild rice would be good. I noticed a leersia in wet meadow edges, but the seeds are small. Acorns are not ripe, nor pine nuts, nor filberts. The inner bark of pine or spruce might be tried. Drank tea until half intoxicated. Man seems to crave a stimulant when anything extraordinary is going on, and this is the only one I use. Billy chews great quantities of tobacco, which I suppose helps to stupefy his misery. We look and listen for the Don every hour. How beautiful upon the mountains [Biblical ref: 'how beautiful upon the mountains are the feet of him who bringeth glad tidings' Isaiah 52:7] his big feet would be!

In the hospitable Sierra, mountain men in general are easily satisfied as to food supplies and bedding. Most of them are heartily content to rough it. The shepherd's bed is often only the bare ground and a pair of blankets, with a stone, a piece of wood, or a pack-saddle for a pillow. In choosing the spot, he shows less care than the dogs, for they usually deliberate, trying for comfort by making many changes, while the shepherd casts himself down anywhere. His food, too, is usually far from delicate, either in kind or in cooking. Beans, bread of any sort, bacon, mutton, dried peaches, and sometimes potatoes and onions, make up his bill-of-fare, the two latter articles being regarded as luxuries on account of their weight – generally in a few days they are gone. Beans are the main standby, portable, simple - although curiously enough a great deal of mystery lies about the bean-pot itself.

No two cooks quite agree on the bean methods: after petting and coaxing the savory mess—well oiled and mellowed with bacon—the proud cook will ask, after dishing out a trial quart or two, "Well, how do you like *my* beans?" Molasses, sugar, or pepper may be used to give desired flavors; or the first water may be poured off and a spoonful or two of ashes or soda added. But no two potfuls are exactly alike. Some are supposed to be spoiled by the moon, by bad luck, by unsuitable soil; or the whole year may be to blame.

Coffee, too, has its marvels in the camp kitchen. A low, complacent grunt follows a mouthful drawn in with a gurgle, and the remark cast forth aimlessly, "That's good coffee." Then another sip and repetition: "*Yes, sir*, that *is* good coffee." As to tea, there are but two kinds, weak and strong, the stronger the better. The only remark heard is, "That tea's weak," otherwise it is good enough. If it has been boiled an hour or two or smoked on a pitchy fire, no matter— who cares for a little tannin or creosote? they make the black beverage all the more attractive to tobacco-tanned palates.

Sheep-camp bread is baked in Dutch ovens, some of it in the form of yeast powder biscuit, an unwholesome sticky, dyspeptic compound. Most of made with sour dough, a handful from each batch being saved to inoculate the next. The oven is simply a cast-iron pot, about five inches deep and from twelve to eighteen inches wide. The oven is slightly heated and rubbed with a piece of tallow or pork rind. The dough is then pressed out against the sides and left to rise. When risen, a shovelful of coals is spread at the side of the fire and the oven set upon them, while another shovelful is placed on top of the lid, which is lifted now and then to check progress. With care good bread may be made in this way, though it is often not good!

At last Don Delaney comes 'doon the lang glen'—hunger vanishes, we turn our eyes to the mountains, and to-morrow we go climbing toward cloudland.

Never while anything is left of me shall this first camp be forgotten. It has fairly grown into me as part of mind and body. The deep hollow, with its majestic trees through which all the wonderful nights the stars poured their beauty; the flowery wildness of the high slope toward Brown's Flat, and its bloom-fragrance descending at the close of still days. The embowered river-reaches with their multitude of voices making melody, the stately flow and rush of currents caressing the dipping sedge-leaves and bushes and mossy stones, ever rejoicing, yet with deep solemn undertones recalling the ocean—the brave little bird ever beside them, singing with sweet human tones among the waltzing foam-bells, and like a blessed evangel explaining God's love.

And the Pilot Peak Ridge, its long withdrawing slopes gracefully braided, reaching from climate to climate and feathered with trees that are the kings of their race, their ranks nobly marshaled spire above spire, waving their arms, tossing their cones like ringing bells—blessed sun-fed mountaineers rejoicing in their strength, a harp for the winds and the sun. The hazel and buckthorn pastures of the deer, the sun-beaten brows purple and yellow with mint and golden-rods, carpeted with chamæbatia, humming with bees. And the dawns and sundowns of these mountain days,—the rose light creeping higher among the stars, changing to daffodil yellow, the level beams streaming across the ridges touching pine after pine, awakening all the mighty host to do gladly their shining day's work. The great sun-gold noons, the alabaster cloud-mountains, the landscape beaming with consciousness like the face of a god. The sunsets, when the trees stood hushed awaiting their good-night blessings. Divine, enduring, unwastable wealth.

CHAPTER IV

TO THE HIGH MOUNTAINS

July 8, 1869. Now away we go toward the topmost mountains. Many still, small voices, as well as the noon thunder, are calling, "Come higher." Farewell blessed dell, woods, streams, birds, squirrels, lizards, and a thousand others. Farewell.

Up through the woods the hoofed locusts streamed beneath a cloud of dust. Almost immediately they seemed to sense new pastures, and rushed wildly ahead like hurrahing flood-waters escaping through a broken dam. A man on each flank kept shouting advice to the leaders, who in their famished condition were behaving like Gadarene swine [biblical ref: Jesus caused the legion of demons inhabiting a lunatic to enter a herd of pigs, which then rushed off a cliff]; two other drivers were busy with stragglers, the Indian, calmly watching for unnoticed wanderers-off; the two dogs running here and there, while the Don, far in the rear, was trying to keep in sight of all his troublesome wealth.

As soon as the boundary of the old eaten-out range was passed, the hungry horde suddenly became calm. Being allowed then to eat their way slowly forward, care was taken only to keep them headed toward the summit of the Merced/Tuolumne divide. Soon the two thousand flattened paunches were bulged out with sweet-pea vines and grass, and the gaunt creatures, more like wolves than sheep, became blandly governable, while the howling drivers changed to gentle shepherds and sauntered in peace.

Toward sundown we reached Hazel Green, on the watershed of the Merced and Tuolumne, where there is a small brook beneath magnificent silver firs and pines. Here, our big fire is blazing like a sunrise, gladly giving back the light slowly sifted from the sunbeams of centuries of summers; and in the glow of that old sunlight how impressively surrounding objects are brought forward in relief! Grasses, larkspurs, columbines, lilies, hazel bushes, and the great trees form a circle around the fire like thoughtful spectators! The night breeze is cool, as all day we have been heading into the home of the clouds. How sweet the air! Here the sugar pine reaches its fullest development, filling every swell and depression almost to the exclusion of other species. A few yellow pines are still to be found, and in cool spots some silver firs; but noble as these are, the sugar pine spreads long protecting arms above them while they wave in recognition.

We have now reached six thousand feet. In the forenoon we passed through manzanita (*Arctostaphylos*), some the largest I have seen. I measured one, the bole of which is four feet at eighteen inches off the ground, where it dissolves into many wide-spreading branches [description of species]. I wonder how old these curious tree-bushes are, probably as old as the great pines. Indians, bears, birds and fat grubs feast on the berries, which look like small rose and green apples. The Indians are said to make a kind of cider out of them. There are many species. Neither wind nor the fires that sweep the woods seldom destroy them utterly, for they rise again from the root, and some of the ridges are seldom touched by fire. I must try to know them better.

I miss my river songs tonight. Here Hazel Creek has a voice like a bird. The wind-tones in the great trees overhead are strangely impressive, but it grows late, and I must to bed. Everybody is asleep. It seems extravagant to spend hours so precious in sleep. "He giveth his beloved sleep." [Biblical ref: Ps 127:2]. Such a pity the poor beloved needs it - to sleep in the midst of eternal, beautiful motion instead of gazing forever, like the stars!

July 9. Exhilarated with the mountain air, I feel like shouting this morning with excess of wild animal joy. The Indian lay down away from the fire last night, having no blanket and nothing on but a pair of blue overalls and a sweaty calico shirt. We gave him some horse-blankets, but he didn't seem to care for them. A fine thing to be independent of clothing where it is so hard to carry. When food is scarce, he can live on whatever comes in his way—a few berries, roots, bird eggs, grasshoppers, black ants, fat wasp or bumblebee larvæ.

Our course today was along the broad top of the main ridge to a hollow beyond Crane Flat. It is covered with the noblest pines and spruces I have yet seen. Sugar pines from six to eight feet in diameter are not uncommon, with a height of two hundred feet or even more. The silver firs (*Abies concolor* and *A. magnifica*) are exceedingly beautiful, especially the *magnifica*, which becomes more abundant the higher we go. It is one of the most notable of the giant conifers of the Sierra. I saw specimens that measured seven feet in diameter and over two hundred feet in height [description of the species].

The other species, *Abies concolor*, attains nearly as great a height and thickness as the *magnifica*, but the branches do not form such regular whorls, nor are they so exactly pinnated or richly leaf-clad. Instead of growing all around the branchlets, the leaves are mostly arranged in two flat horizontal rows. The cones and seeds are like those of the *magnifica* in form but less than half as large. The bark of the *magnifica* is reddish purple and closely furrowed, that of the *concolor* gray and widely furrowed. A noble pair.

At Crane Flat we climbed a thousand feet or more in just two miles, the forest growing more dense and the silvery *magnifica* fir forming a greater portion of the whole. Crane Flat is a meadow with a wide sandy border lying on the top of the divide. It is often visited by migrating blue cranes to rest and feed, hence the name. It is about half a mile long, draining into the Merced, sedgy in the middle, with a margin bright with lilies, etc [list of species]. About a mile from the north end of the flat there is a grove of *Sequoia gigantea*, the king of all the conifers. Furthermore, the Douglas spruce (*Pseudotsuga Douglasii*) and *Libocedrus decurrens*, and a few two-leaved pines, occur here and there, forming a small part of the forest. Three pines, two silver firs, one Douglas spruce, one sequoia—all of them, except the two-leaved pine, colossal trees - are found here together, an assemblage of conifers unrivaled on the globe.

We passed a number of charming garden-like meadows lying on top of the divide or imbedded in the glorious forest. Some are taken up chiefly with the tall white-flowered *Veratrum Californicum*, with boat-shaped leaves about a foot long, eight or ten inches wide, and veined like those of cypripedium—a robust, hearty, liliaceous plant, fond of water and determined to be seen. [List of species].

One might reasonably look for a wall of fire to fence such gardens. So extravagant is Nature with her choicest treasures, spending plant beauty like sunshine. The beauty of lilies falls on angels and men, bears and squirrels, wolves and sheep, birds and bees, but as far as I have seen, man alone, and his animals, destroy these gardens. Awkward, lumbering bears, the Don tells me, love to wallow in them in hot weather, and deer with their sharp feet cross them again and again, sauntering and feeding, yet never a lily have I seen spoiled by them.

The trees round about them seem as perfect in beauty and form as the lilies, their boughs whorled like lily leaves in exact order. Lying beneath the firs, it is glorious to see them dipping their spires in the starry sky, the sky like one vast lily meadow in bloom! How can I close my eyes on so precious a night?

July 10. A Douglas squirrel, peppery autocrat of the woods, is barking overhead this morning, and the small forest birds are out on sunny branches along the edge of the meadow getting warm. How charming the sprightly confident ways of these little feathered people of the trees! How helpless should we find ourselves should we try to set a table for them of such buds, seeds, insects, etc., as would keep them in the pure wild health they enjoy! Not a headache or any other ache amongst them, I guess. As for the irrepressible Douglas squirrels, one never thinks of the possibility of hunger, sickness or death; rather they seem like stars above chance or change, even though we may see them at times working hard for a living.

On through the forest ever higher we go, a cloud of dust dimming the way, thousands of feet trampling leaves and flowers, but in this mighty wilderness they seem but a feeble band, and a thousand gardens will escape their blighting touch. They cannot hurt the trees, though some of the seedlings suffer, but should the woolly locusts be greatly multiplied, on account of dollar value, then the forests, too, may in time be destroyed. Only the sky will then be safe, though hid from view by dust and smoke, incense of a bad sacrifice. Poor sheep, in great part misbegotten, without good right to be, semi-manufactured, made by man, born out of time and place, yet their voices are strangely human and call out one's pity.

Our way is still along the Merced and Tuolumne divide, the streams on our right going to the Yosemite River, those on our left to the songful Tuolumne, slipping through sunny carex and lily meadows, and breaking into song down the ravines. A more tuneful set of streams surely nowhere exists.

All day I have been gazing in growing admiration at the noble groups of the magnificent silver fir. The woods above Crane Flat are still quite open, letting in sunshine on the brown needle-strewn ground. The dullest eye in the world must surely be quickened by such temple groves as these.

Fortunately the sheep need little attention, as they are driven slowly and allowed to nibble as they like. Since leaving Hazel Green we have been following the Yosemite trail; visitors to the famous valley coming by way of Coulterville and Chinese Camp pass this way — the two trails uniting at Crane Flat — and enter the valley on the north side. Another trail enters on the south side via Mariposa. The tourists we saw (in parties of from three to twenty) were mounted on mules or small mustangs. A strange show they made, winding single file through the solemn woods in gaudy attire, scaring the wild creatures, and one might fancy that even the great pines would groan. But what may we say of us and the flock?

We are now camped at Tamarack Flat, within four or five miles of the lower end of Yosemite. Here is another fine meadow with a deep, clear stream gliding through it, its banks rounded and beveled with a thatch of dipping sedges. The flat is named after the two-leaved pine (*Pinus contorta*, var. *Murrayana*), [description of the species].

July 11. The Don has gone ahead to spy out the land to the north of Yosemite in search of the best central camping point. Higher than this we cannot yet go, for the upper pastures are still buried in heavy winter snow. Many a glorious ramble I'll have along the top of the walls, and what landscapes I shall find!

We are now about seven thousand feet, and must pile coats and extra clothing on top of our blankets. Tamarack Creek is icy cold, champagne water. It is bank-full with silent speed, but only a few hundred yards below our camp the ground is bare, with boulders, and few trees in the cracks. The boulders, many of them very large, are not in piles or scattered like rubbish; they mostly occur singly, and are lying on a clean pavement on which the sunshine falls in a glare that contrasts with the leafy woods. Strange to say, these boulders were brought from a distance, as difference in color and composition shows; nor have they stirred since first they arrived. The largest are twenty or thirty feet in diameter, and with what tool were they quarried and carried? On the pavement we find its marks. The surface is scored and striated in a rigidly parallel way, indicating that the region has been overswept by a glacier from the northeastward, producing a strange, raw, wiped appearance, and dropping whatever boulders it chanced to be carrying at the time it was melted at the close of the Glacial Period. A fine discovery this. As for the forests we have been passing through, they are probably growing on moraines of different sorts, now in great part disintegrated by post-glacial weathering.

Out of the grassy meadow and down over this ice-planed granite runs the glad young Tamarack Creek, rejoicing on its way to the Merced Canyon, a few miles below Yosemite, falling more than three thousand feet in only two miles.

All the Merced streams are wonderful singers, and Yosemite is the centre where the main tributaries meet. From a point about half a mile from our camp we can see into the lower end of the famous valley, with its wonderful cliffs and groves. How vast it seems, how short human life when we happen to think of it, and how little we may learn, however hard we try! Some of the external beauty is always in sight, enough to keep every fibre of us tingling, though the methods of creation may lie beyond our ken. Sing on, brave Tamarack Creek, fresh from your snowy fountains, plash and swirl and dance to your fate in the sea!

Have greatly enjoyed all this huge day, steeping in the mountain influences, sketching, noting, pressing flowers, drinking ozone and Tamarack water. Found the white fragrant Washington lily, the finest of all the Sierra lilies. Its bulbs are buried in shaggy chaparral tangles for safety from pawing bears; and its magnificent panicles sway over the rough snow-pressed bushes, while big, blunt-nosed bees mumble in its polleny bells. A lovely flower, worth going hungry and footsore endless miles to see. The whole world seems richer now that I have found this plant in so noble a landscape.

A log house serves to mark a claim to the Tamarack meadow, which may become valuable as a station in case travel to Yosemite should greatly increase. Belated parties occasionally stop here. A white man with an Indian woman is holding possession of the place.

Sauntered up the meadow about sundown, out of sight of camp and sheep and all human mark, into the deep peace of the solemn old woods, everything glowing with Heaven's unquenchable enthusiasm.

July 12. The Don has returned, and again we go on pilgrimage. "Looking over the Yosemite Creek country," he said, "from the hilltops you see nothing but rocks and patches of trees; but down into the rocky desert [there are] no end of small grassy banks and meadows, and so the country is not half so lean as it looks. There we'll till the snow is melted from the upper country."

I was glad to hear that the high snow made a stay in the Yosemite region necessary. What fine times I shall have sketching, studying plants and rocks, and scrambling about the brink of the great valley alone!

We saw another party of Yosemite tourists today. These travelers seem to care little for the glorious objects about them, though enough to endure the long rides. And when they are fairly within the mighty temple walls and hear the psalms of the falls, they will forget themselves and become devout. Blessed, indeed, every pilgrim in these holy mountains!

We moved along the Mono Trail, and early in the afternoon we camped on the bank of Cascade Creek. The Mono Trail crosses the range by the Bloody Canyon Pass to gold mines near the north end of Mono Lake. These mines were reported to be rich when first discovered, and a grand rush took place. Bridges were built over streams unfordable due to softness of the bottom; sections of fallen trees cut out; lanes made through thickets to admit bulky packs; but over the greater trail not a shovelful of earth has been moved.

The woods now are almost wholly *Abies magnifica*, the companion species, *concolor*, being mostly left on lower slopes. No words can do anything like justice to this noble tree. At one place many had fallen during heavy wind, owing to the loose sandy soil, which is mostly disintegrated moraine material.

The sheep are lying in a bare rocky spot, chewing the cud. Cooking is going on, appetites growing keener daily. No lowlander can appreciate the mountain appetite, and the facility with which heavy food called "grub" is disposed of. All activities seem alike delightful, and one feels inclined to shout lustily on rising - like a crowing cock. Sleep and digestion as clear as the air. Spicy boughs for bedding we shall have to-night, and a glorious lullaby from this creek: one continuous bouncing, dancing, white bloom of cascades. At last it finishes leaps grandly three hundred feet or more to the bottom of the main Yosemite canyon. These falls rival the far-famed Yosemite falls. Never shall I forget these glad cascade songs, booming, roaring, a keen, silvery clash of cool water rushing exultingly beneath irised spray; or white in the darkness, its multitude of voices sounding still more sublime.

Here I find the little water ouzel as much at home as any woodland linnet, delighting more the more boisterous the stream. The dizzy precipices and the thunder tones of the sheer falls are awe inspiring, but there is nothing awful about this little bird. Its song is sweet and low, and all its gestures amid the loud uproar bespeak strength and joy. Contemplating these darlings of Nature on the brink of savage streams, Samson's riddle comes to mind, "Out of the strong cometh forth sweetness." [Biblical ref: Judg. 14:14. Samson killed a lion. On returning to the carcase he found a beehive within it – he used this as the basis for a riddle].

July 13. Our course all day has been eastward over the rim of Yosemite Creek basin and down about halfway to the bottom. We have camped on a sheet of glacier-polished granite. Saw the tracks of a very large bear, and the Don talked of bears. I said I should like to follow the maker of these immense tracks him for days, to learn something of the life of this master beast. Lambs, the Don said, that never saw a bear, snort and run in terror when they catch the scent, showing how fully they have inherited a knowledge of their enemy. Hogs, mules, horses, and cattle are afraid of bears, and are seized with ungovernable terror when they approach. Hogs in hundreds-strong droves are frequently driven to pasture in the foothills of the Coast Range and Sierra when acorns are abundant. If a bear comes to the range they promptly leave it, emigrating in a body, usually in the night, the keepers being powerless.

Sheep, on the other hand, simply scatter in the brush and await their fate. Mules flee like the wind with or without riders when they see a bear. Picketed mules will sometimes break their necks in trying to break their ropes. Of hogs bears are particularly fond, bolting small ones, bones and all. Mr. Delaney assured me that all bears in the Sierra are very shy, and that hunters found it more difficult to get within range of them than of deer or other animals. If I was anxious to see them I should have to wait with endless Indian patience and committment.

Night is coming on, the gray rock waves are growing dim in the twilight. How young this region appears! Had the sweeping ice sheet vanished but yesterday, its traces about our camp could hardly be more distinct. The horses and sheep and all of us, indeed, slipped on the smoothest places.

July 14. How deathlike is sleep in this mountain air, and how quick the awakening! A calm dawn, yellow and purple, then floods of sungold, making every thing tingle and glow.

In an hour or two we came to Yosemite Creek, the stream that makes the greatest of all the Yosemite falls. It is about forty feet wide at the

Mono Trail crossing, and now about four feet deep, flowing about three miles an hour. The distance to where it makes its tremendous plunge, is only about two miles. Calm, nearly silent, it glides with stately gestures, a dense growth of the slender two-leaved pine along its banks, and a fringe of willow, purple spirea, sedges, daisies, lilies, and columbines. Some of the sedges and willow boughs dip into the current, and just outside of the close ranks of trees there is a sunny flat of washed gravelly sand maybe deposited by some ancient flood.

This swathe is covered with millions of erethrea, eriogonum, and oxytheca, punctuated by rosettes of *Spraguea umbellata*. Back of this is a wavy upsloping plain of solid granite, so smoothly ice-polished in many places that it glistens like glass. In soil-poor hollows are patches of the two-leaved pine, looking rather scrawny. Also a few short, isolated junipers (*Juniperus occidentalis*, with bright cinnamon-colored bark and gray foliage, a sturdy storm-enduring mountaineer of a tree, possibly living on more than a thousand years.

At the head of the basin groups of cloud domes are rising above the wavelike ridges, and some picturesque castellated masses of silver fir, indicating deposits of fertile soil. What rich excursions one could make in this well-defined basin! Its glacial sculptings, how marvelous they seem, how noble the studies they offer! I tremble with excitement in these mountain sublimities, but can only gaze and wonder, half hoping I may be able to study and learn in years to come.

The drivers and dogs had a lively time getting the sheep across the creek, the second large stream they have been compelled to cross without a bridge. A close crowd was driven against the bank, but not one would launch away. Don and the shepherd rushed through the dense frightened crowd to stampede those in front, but this would only cause a break backward into the stream-bank trees, to then scatter up over the rocky pavement. Again and again the compacted mass would break away, amid wild shouting and barking that marred the music of the falls, to which visitors from all the globe were listening. "Hold them there! Now hold them there!" shouted the Don; "the front ranks will soon tire of the pressure, and be glad to take to the water, then all will jump in and cross in a hurry." But they did nothing of the kind; they only broke back in scores, leaving the beauty of the banks sadly trampled.

A lamb was carried across and tied to a bush on the opposite bank, where it cried piteously. But though greatly concerned, the mother only called it back. That play having failed, we feared we should be forced to cross the wide-spread smaller tributaries of the creek in succession. This would only advantage me, for I was eager to see the sources of so famous a stream. Don Quixote began a sort of siege by cutting down slender pines on the bank and building a corral barely large enough to hold the jammed-in flock.

In a few hours this enclosure was completed, and the silly animals were rammed hard against the water's brink. The Don, forcing a way through the compacted mass, pitched a few unfortunates into the stream by main strength; but instead of crossing over, they swam about close to the bank, making desperate attempts to get back. Then a dozen or more were shoved off, and the Don, tall as a crane and a good wader, jumped in after them, seized a struggling wether, and dragged it to the opposite shore. But it jumped straight back into the stream and swam back to its frightened companions.

Pan with his pipes would have had no better luck. We were now baffled. Calling a council, the dripping Don declared that we might as well camp here and let the besieged flock grow hungry and come to their senses. In a few minutes after being thus let alone, an adventurer in the foremost rank plunged in and swam bravely to the farther shore. Then suddenly all rushed in pell-mell together, trampling each other under water, while we tried to hold them back. The Don jumped into the thick of the drowning mass and shoved them right and left like floating timber. The current helped, a long bent column was soon formed, and in a few minutes all were over. They began baaing and feeding as if nothing had happened. That none were drowned – I had fully expected that hundreds would gain the romantic fate of being swept into Yosemite over the highest waterfall in the world.

As the day was spent, we camped back from the ford, and let the dripping flock scatter and feed. The wool is dry now, and calm, cud-chewing peace has fallen on all the band. I have seen fish driven out of the water with less ado than was made in driving these animals into it. Sheep brain must surely be poor stuff. Compare the performances of deer swimming quietly across rapid rivers, and from island to island in lakes; or even with the squirrels that, as the story goes, cross the Mississippi River on selected chips, with tails comfortably trimmed to the breeze. A sheep can hardly be called an animal; an entire flock is required to make one foolish individual.

CHAPTER V

THE YOSEMITE

July 15, 1869. Followed the Mono Trail up the eastern rim of the basin nearly to its summit, then turned off southward to a small shallow valley that extends to the edge of the Yosemite, which we reached about noon to make camp. After lunch I hastened to high ground, and from the top of the west side of Indian Canyon gained the noblest view of the summit peaks I have ever yet enjoyed. Nearly all the upper basin of the Merced was shown, with its sublime domes and canyons, dark upsweeping forests, and glorious array of white peaks deep in the sky, every feature radiating beauty that pours into us like heat from fire. Sunshine over all; no breath of wind to stir the brooding calm.

Never before had I seen so boundless an affluence of sublime mountain beauty. The most extravagant description I might give would not so much as hint at its grandeur and the spiritual glow that covered it. I shouted and jumped about in a wild burst of ecstasy, much to the astonishment of St. Bernard Carlo.

A brown bear, too, had been a spectator of the show I had made of myself, for I started one from a thicket of brush. He ran away very fast, tumbling over the tops of the tangled manzanita bushes in his haste. Carlo, his ears depressed as if afraid, kept looking me in the face, expecting me to pursue and shoot.

Following the ridge as it graded to the south, I came to the brow of that massive cliff that stands between Indian Canyon and Yosemite Falls, and here the valley came into view through its whole extent. The noble walls—sculptured into endless variety of domes and gables, spires and precipices—all a-tremble with the thunder of the falling water. The level bottom was dressed like a garden—sunny meadows, groves of pine and oak; the river of Mercy [Merced] sweeping through and flashing back the sunbeams. The great Tissiack, or Half-Dome, rising to a height of nearly a mile, is nobly proportioned, the most impressive of all the rocks, holding the eye in devout admiration, recalling the eye repeatedly from the other wonders. Thousands of years have they stood in the sky exposed to rain, snow, frost and earth tremor, yet they still wear the bloom of youth.

I rambled westward; the rim rounded off on the very brink, so that it is not easy to find places where one may look clear down the rock face. When such places were found, and I had set my feet and drawn my body erect, I could not help fearing that the rock might split and let me down more than three thousand feet. Still, my limbs did not tremble, nor did I feel uncertain as to their reliability. Seeing the rock faults below me, I would say, "Now don't go out on the verge again." But in the face of Yosemite, caution is in vain; under its spell one's body seems to go where it likes.

After a mile or so of this memorable cliff work I approached Yosemite Creek in its narrow channel, singing the last of its mountain songs on its way to its fate - down half a mile in showy foam to another world, to be lost in the Merced, where all is different. Emerging from its last gorge, it glides in wide lacy rapids down into a pool where it composes its gray, agitated waters before taking the grand plunge, then slowly slipping over the lip of the pool basin, it descends another glossy slope with rapidly accelerated speed to the cliff, and with sublime, fateful confidence springs out free in the air.

I took off my shoes and stockings and worked my way alongside the rushing flood, keeping my feet and hands firmly on the polished rock. The booming, roaring water, rushing past close to my head, was very exciting. I had expected that the sloping apron would end with the perpendicular valley wall, and that from the foot of it, where it is less steep, I would be able to lean out to see the behavior of the fall all the way down to the bottom. But there was yet another small brow over which I could not see, apparently too steep for mortal feet. Scanning it, I saw a narrow shelf about three inches wide on the very brink, just wide enough for one's heels. But there seemed to be no way of reaching it over the steep brow. At length, I spied an irregular edge of rock back from the margin of the torrent. It was the only way. But the slope beside it looked dangerously smooth and steep; I therefore concluded not to venture farther, but did nonetheless.

Tufts of artemisia were growing in clefts of the rock nearby, and I filled my mouth with the bitter leaves, hoping they might help to prevent giddiness. Then, with a caution unusual for me, I crept down to the little ledge, got my heels well planted on it, then shuffled in a horizontal direction about thirty feet, close to the outplunging white current. Here I obtained a perfect view into the heart of the snowy, chanting throng of comet-like streamers into which the body of the fall soon separates.

I was not distinctly conscious of danger. The tremendous grandeur of the fall, acting at close range, smothered the sense of fear - one's body takes keen care on its own account. How long I remained down there, or how I returned I can hardly tell. I got back to camp about dark, enjoying triumphant exhilaration, followed by dull weariness. Hereafter I'll try to keep from such nerve-straining places. Yet such a day is well worth venturing for. My first view of the High Sierra, first view looking down into Yosemite, the death song of Yosemite Creek, and its flight over the vast cliff, each one of these is great life-long landscape fortune—a most memorable day of days— enjoyment enough to kill if that were possible.

July 16. My enjoyments yesterday, especially at the head of the fall, were too great for good sleep. Kept starting up last night in a nervous terror, fancying that the foundation of the mountain we were camped on was falling into Yosemite Valley. The nerve strain had been too great, and again and again I dreamed I was rushing through the air above a glorious avalanche of water and rocks. One time, jumping up, I said, "This time it is real—all must die, and where could mountaineer find a more glorious death!"

Left camp soon after sunrise for an all-day ramble eastward. Crossed the head of Indian Basin, forested with *Abies magnifica*, underbrush mostly *Ceanothus cordulatus* and manzanita, a mixture not easily trampled over or penetrated, for the ceanothus is thorny and grows in dense snow-pressed masses, and the manzanita has exceedingly crooked, stubborn branches. From the head of the canyon continued on past North Dome into the basin of Dome or Porcupine Creek. Here are many fine meadows embedded in the woods, gay with *Lilium parvum* and its companions; the elevation, about eight thousand feet, seems to be best suited for it—saw specimens a foot or two higher than me. Had more magnificent views of the upper mountains and of the great South Dome, said to be the grandest rock in the world. Well it may be: a wonderfully impressive monument, its lines exquisite in fineness, finished like the finest work of art, and seemingly alive.

July 17. Camp made today in a magnificent silver fir grove at the head of a stream that flows into Yosemite via Indian Canyon. Here we'll stay several weeks—a fine location from which to make excursions. Glorious days I'll have sketching, pressing plants, studying the topography and the wild animals, our happy fellow mortals. But the vast mountains in the distance, shall I ever know them, shall I be allowed to enter their midst and dwell with them?

We were pelted about noon by a short, heavy rainstorm, sublime thunder reverberating among the canyons—some strokes nearby, ringing in the tense air with startling keenness, while the distant peaks loomed gloriously through the cloud fringes and sheets of rain.

Now the storm is past, and the fresh washed air is full of the essences of the flower gardens and groves. Winter storms in Yosemite must be glorious. May I see them!

Have got my bed made in our new camp - sumptuous and deliciously fragrant, most of it *magnifica* fir plumes, of course, with a variety of sweet flowers in the pillow. Hope to sleep tonight without tottering nerve-dreams. Watched a deer eating ceanothus leaves and twigs.

July 18. Slept pretty well; the valley walls did not seem to fall, though I still fancied myself at the brink, alongside the white, plunging flood. Strange the danger of that adventure should be more troublesome now that I am in the bosom of the peaceful woods, than it was while I was on the brink of it.

Bears seem to be common here, judging by their tracks. About noon we had another rainstorm with keen startling thunder, the strokes fading into low bass rolling and muttering in the distance. For a few minutes the rain came in a grand torrent like a waterfall, then hail; some of the hailstones an inch in diameter, irregular in form, like those oftentimes seen in Wisconsin. Carlo watched them with intelligent astonishment as they came pelting and thrashing through the quivering branches of the trees. The cloud scenery sublime. Afternoon calm, sunful, and clear, with delicious freshness and fragrance from the firs and flowers and steaming ground.

July 19. Watching the sunrise: a pale rose and purple sky changing softly to daffodil yellow and white, sunbeams pouring through the passes between the peaks and over Yosemite's domes, making their edges burn; the silver firs in the middle ground catching the glow on their spiry tops, and our camp grove fill and thrill with the glorious light. Everything awakening alert and joyful; the birds begin to stir and innumerable insect people. Deer quietly withdraw into leafy hiding-places in the chaparral; the dew vanishes, flowers spread their petals, every pulse beats high, every cell rejoices, the very rocks seem to thrill with life. The whole landscape glows like a human face in a glory of enthusiasm [Gk: enthousiasmos = filled with spirit], and the blue sky, pale around the horizon, bends peacefully down over all like one vast flower.

About noon, as usual, big bossy cumuli began to grow above the forest, and the rainstorm pouring from them is the most imposing I have yet seen. The silvery lightning lances are longer than usual, and the thunder gloriously impressive, speaking with such tremendous energy it would seem that an entire mountain is being shattered at every stroke, but probably only a few trees are being shattered. At last the ringing strokes are succeeded by deep low tones that grow gradually fainter as they roll afar into the recesses of the echoing mountains, where they seem to be welcomed home. Then another and another peal follows in quick succession, perchance splitting some giant pine into long slivers scattered to all points of the compass. Now comes the rain with corresponding extravagant grandeur, covering the ground in a sheet of flowing water, a transparent film fitted like a skin upon the rugged anatomy of the landscape, making the rocks glitter, gathering in the ravines, flooding the streams, and making them shout and boom in reply to the thunder.

How interesting to trace the history of a single raindrop! It is not long, geologically speaking, as we have seen, since the first raindrops fell on the newborn leafless Sierra landscapes [since the end of the Ice Age]. How different the lot of those falling now! Happy the showers that fall on so fair a wilderness, scarce a single drop can fail to find a beautiful spot on the tops of the peaks, shining glacier pavements, on great smooth domes, on forests and brushy moraines, plashing, pattering, laving. Some go to the high snowy fountains to swell their well-saved stores; some to the lakes, washing the mountain windows, patting their smooth glassy levels, making dimples and spray; some into the cascades, as if eager to join in their dance and beat their foam yet finer; good luck for the happy mountain raindrops, each one of them a high waterfall in itself, descending from the cliffs and hollows of the clouds to the cliffs and hollows of the rocks, out of the sky-thunder into the thunder of the falling rivers.

Some, falling on meadows and bogs, creep silently out of sight to the grass roots, hiding softly as in a nest, slipping, oozing here and there, seeking their appointed work. Some, descending through the spires of the woods, sift spray through the shining needles, whispering peace and good cheer to each one of them. Some drops with happy aim glint on the sides of crystals—quartz, garnet, zircon, feldspar—patter on grains of gold and heavy way-worn nuggets; some, with blunt plap-plap and low bass drumming, fall on the broad leaves of veratrum, saxifrage, cypripedium.

Some happy drops fall straight into the cups of flowers, kissing the lips of lilies. How far they have to go, how many cups to fill, cups holding half a drop as well as lake basins between the hills, each replenished with equal care, every drop in all the blessed throng a silvery newborn star with lake and grove, valley and mountain, all that the landscape holds reflected in its crystal depths, God's messenger, angel of love sent on its way with majesty and display of power that make man's greatest shows ridiculous. [Possibly Muir at his most florid!]

Storm now over, the sky is clear, the last rolling thunder is spent on the peaks, and where are the raindrops now—what has become of all the shining throng? In winged vapor some are already hastening back to the sky, some into the plants, creeping through invisible doors into the rooms of cells, some are locked in ice crystals, some in rock crystals, some in porous moraines to keep their small springs flowing, some journeying on in the rivers to join the larger raindrop of the ocean. From form to form, beauty to beauty, all are speeding on with love's enthusiasm, singing with the stars the eternal song of creation.

July 20. Fine calm morning; air tense and clear; not the slightest breeze astir; everything shining, both rocks and plants, each receiving its portion of irised dewdrops and sunshine like living creatures getting their breakfast, their dew manna coming down from the starry sky like swarms of smaller stars. [Biblical ref: God caused 'manna' – a food from heaven, to fall in the desert to feed the

Israelites on the way to the promised land, having left Egypt]. How wondrous fine are the particles in showers of dew! What pains are taken to keep this wilderness in health—showers of snow, showers of rain, showers of dew, floods of light, floods of invisible vapor, clouds, winds, all sorts of weather, interaction of plant on plant, animal on animal, etc., beyond thought! How fine Nature's methods! How deeply with beauty is beauty overlaid! the ground covered with crystals, the crystals with mosses and lichens and low-spreading grasses and flowers, these with larger plants leaf over leaf with ever-changing color and form, the broad palms of the firs outspread over these, the azure dome over all like a bell-flower, and star above star.

Yonder stands the South Dome, its crown high above our camp, though its base is four thousand feet below us; a most noble rock, it seems full of thought, clothed with living light, no sense of dead stone about it, all spiritualized, neither heavy looking nor light, steadfast in serene strength like a god.

Our shepherd is a queer character - hard to place in this wilderness. His bed is made in red, dry-rot dust beside a log in the south wall of the corral. Here he lies in his wonderful everlasting clothing, wrapped in a red blanket, breathing not only decayed wood dust but also that of the corral, as if determined to take ammoniacal snuff all night after chewing tobacco all day. He carries a heavy six-shooter one side on his belt and his luncheon on the other. The ancient cloth in which fresh-fried meat is tied serves as a filter through which fat and gravy juices drip down his right hip and leg in clustering stalactites. This oleaginous formation is soon diffused and rubbed evenly into his scanty apparel by all his actions, making shirt and trousers water-tight and shiny.

His trousers, in particular, have become so adhesive with the mixed fat and resin that pine needles, thin flakes of bark, hair, mica scales and minute grains of sand, feathers, moth and butterfly wings, whole or parts of innumerable insects; with flower petals, pollen - indeed bits of all plants, animals, and minerals of the region adhere to them and are safely embedded, so that far from being a naturalist he collects fragmentary specimens of everything and becomes richer than he knows. His specimens are kept passably fresh by the purity of the air and the resiny, bituminous beds into which they are pressed. Man is a microcosm, at least our shepherd is, or rather his trousers. These precious overalls are never taken off, and nobody knows how old they are, though one may guess by their thickness and concentric structure. Instead of wearing thin they wear thick, and in their stratification have no small geological significance.

Besides herding the sheep, Billy is the butcher, while I have agreed to wash the few iron and tin utensils and make the bread. Then, these small duties done, by the time the sun is fairly above the mountain-tops I am beyond the flock, free to revel in the wilderness all the big immortal days.

Sketching on the North Dome. It commands views of nearly all the valley besides a few of the high mountains. I would fain draw everything in sight—rock, tree, and leaf. But little can I do beyond mere outlines—marks with meanings like words, readable only to myself; yet I sharpen my pencils and work on as if others might possibly benefit. Whether these pictures are to vanish like fallen leaves or go to friends like letters, matters not; for little can they tell to those who have not seen similar wildness, and like a language learned it. No pain here, no dull empty hours, no fear of the past, no fear of the future. These blessed mountains are so compactly filled with God's beauty, no petty personal experience has room to be. Drinking this champagne water is pure pleasure, so is breathing the living air, and every movement of limbs is pleasure, while the whole body seems to feel beauty when exposed to it as it feels the camp-fire or sunshine, entering not by the eyes alone, but equally through all one's flesh like radiant heat, making a passionate glow not explainable.

One's body then seems homogeneous throughout, sound as a crystal. Perched like a fly on this Yosemite dome, I gaze and sketch and bask, often settling into dumb admiration without definite hope of ever learning much, yet with the unresting effort that lies at the door of hope, humbly prostrate before the vast display of God's power, and eager to offer self-denial with eternal toil to learn any lesson in the divine manuscript.

It is easier to feel than to realize, or in any way explain, Yosemite grandeur. Sheer precipices three thousand feet high are fringed with tall trees growing close like grass on the brow of a lowland hill, and extending along the feet of these precipices a ribbon of meadow a mile wide and seven or eight long, that seems like a strip a farmer might mow in less than a day. Waterfalls, five hundred to two thousand feet high, so subordinated to the mighty cliffs over which they pour they seem like wisps of smoke, though their voices make the rocks tremble. The mountains, too, along the eastern sky, and the domes in front of them, and the succession of smooth rounded waves between, swelling higher, with dark woods in their hollows, serene in exuberant bulk and beauty, are as a subdued subordinate feature in the vast harmonious landscape.

Every attempt to appreciate any one feature is beaten down by the overwhelming influence of all the others. And, as if this were not enough, lo! in the sky rises another rugged mountain range with topography as substantial as the one beneath it—snowy peaks and domes and shadowy Yosemite valleys—another version of the Sierra, a new creation heralded by a thunder-storm. How devoutly wild is Nature in the midst of her tenderness!—painting lilies, watering them, going from flower to flower like a gardener while building rock and cloud mountains full of lightning and rain. Gladly we run for shelter beneath an overhanging cliff and examine the reassuring ferns and mosses, gentle love tokens growing in cracks and chinks. Daisies, too, and ivesias, confiding wild children of light, too small to fear. To these one's heart goes home, and the voices of the storm become gentle. Now the sun breaks forth and fragrant steam arises. The birds are out singing on the edges of the groves. The west is flaming in gold and purple, ready for the ceremony of the sunset, and back I go to camp with my notes and pictures, the best of them printed in my mind as dreams. A fruitful day, without measured beginning or ending. A terrestrial eternity. A gift of good God.

Wrote to my mother and a few friends, mountain hints to each. They seem as near as if within touch. The deeper the solitude the less the sense of loneliness, and the nearer our friends. Now bread and tea, fir bed and good-night to Carlo, a look at the sky lilies, and death sleep until the dawn of another Sierra to-morrow.

July 21. Sketching on the Dome—no rain; clouds at noon about quarter-filled the sky, casting fine shadows on the white mountains at the stream heads, and a soothing cover over the heated gardens.

Saw a common housefly, a grasshopper and a brown bear. The fly and grasshopper paid me a merry visit on the top of the Dome, and I visited the bear in a little meadow between the Dome and the camp. He was standing alert among the flowers as if willing to be seen to advantage. I had not gone more than half a mile from camp this morning, when Carlo, trotting a few yards ahead of me, came to a sudden standstill. Down went tail and ears and forward went his nose. He seemed to be saying, "Ha, what's this? A bear, I guess."

Then a cautious small advance, setting his feet down softly like a cat, and questing the air till all doubt vanished. He came back to me, looked me in the face, and with his speaking eyes reported a bear; then led on softly, like an experienced hunter, not to make the slightest noise; and frequently looking back as if whispering, "Yes, it's a bear; come and I'll show you."

Presently we came to where sunbeams streamed through purple shafts of the firs - we were nearing an open spot, and here Carlo came behind me, evidently sure that the bear was very near. I crept to a low ridge of boulders on the edge of a narrow meadow, feeling pretty sure the bear must be there. I was anxious to get a good look at the sturdy mountaineer without alarming him. Drawing myself up noiselessly behind a large tree I peered out carefully, and there stood neighbor Bruin within a stone's throw, his hips covered by tall grass and flowers, and his front feet on the trunk of a fallen fir, which raised his head so high he seemed to be standing erect.

He had not yet seen me, but was very attentive, showing that he was aware of our approach. I tried to learn what I could about him, fearing he would see me and run away. I had been told that this sort of bear, the cinnamon, always ran from his bad brother man, never showing fight unless wounded or in defense of young. He made a telling picture standing alert in the forest garden. How well he played his part, harmonizing with the trunks of the trees and lush vegetation. After noting the sharp muzzle, the shaggy hair on his broad chest, the erect ears nearly buried in hair, and the heavy way he moved his head, I thought I should like to see him run, so I made a sudden rush at him, shouting and swinging my hat to frighten him, expecting to see him make haste to get away. But to my dismay he did not show any sign of running. On the contrary, he stood his ground ready to fight, thrust forward his lowered head, and looked sharply and fiercely at me.

Suddenly began to fear, but I was afraid to run and therefore, like the bear, held my ground. We stood staring at each other within a dozen yards or so, while I fervently hoped that the power of the human eye over wild beasts would prove as great as it is said to be. How long our awful interview lasted, I don't know; but at length he pulled his huge paws down off the log, and with magnificent deliberation turned and walked leisurely up the meadow, stopping to look back over his shoulder, then moving on, evidently neither fearing me nor trusting me. He weighed probably about five hundred pounds, a broad, rusty bundle of ungovernable wildness, a happy fellow whose lines have fallen in pleasant places [biblical ref: Ps 16:6 'the [boundary] lines are fallen for me in pleasant places,' referring to the dividing of land by measuring ropes and by lot in ancient Israel].

The flowery glade in which I saw him, framed like a picture, is one of the best I have yet discovered, a conservatory of precious plant people: tall lilies swinging their bells over that bear's back, geraniums, larkspurs, columbines, and daisies brushing his sides. A place for angels, one would say, instead of bears.

In the great canyons Bruin reigns supreme. Happy fellow, whom no famine can reach while one of his thousand kinds of food is spared him. His bread is sure at all seasons, ranged on the mountain shelves like stores in a pantry. Up and down he climbs, enjoying each in turn in different climates, as if he had journeyed to other countries to enjoy their varied productions. I should like to know my hairy brothers better—though after this particular Yosemite neighbor had sauntered out of sight this morning, I reluctantly went back to camp for the rifle to shoot him in defense of the flock. Fortunately I couldn't find him, and after tracking him a mile or two towards Mount Hoffman I bade him Godspeed and gladly returned to my work on the Yosemite Dome.

The housefly also seemed at home and buzzed about me as I sat sketching, enjoying my bear interview in memory. I wonder what draws houseflies so far up the mountains, heavy gross feeders as they are, sensitive to cold, and fond of domestic ease. How have they been distributed across seas and deserts and mountains - usually so influential in determining the boundaries of all species? Beetles and butterflies are sometimes restricted to small areas, even the different zones of one mountain may have their own peculiar species. But the housefly seems to be everywhere. I wonder if any island in mid-ocean is flyless. The bluebottle is abundant in these Yosemite woods, ever ready with a marvelous store of eggs to make all dead flesh fly. Bumblebees are here, well fed on boundless nectar and pollen. The honeybee, though abundant in the foothills, has not yet got so high. It is only a few years since the first swarm was brought to California.

A queer and jolly fellow is the grasshopper! Up the mountains he comes on excursions, how high I don't know, but at least as far and high as Yosemite tourists. I was much interested with the hearty enjoyment of the one that danced and sang for me on the Dome this afternoon. He seemed brimful of glad, hilarious energy, manifested by springing repeatedly into the air to a height of up to thirty feet, making a sharp musical rattle just as the lowest point was reached. Up and down a dozen times or so he danced and sang, then alighted to rest, then up and at it again. [Probably a mating display]. The curves he described in the air in diving and rattling resembled those made by cords hanging loosely and attached at the same height at the ends, the loops nearly covering each other. [These curves are known in architecture as 'catenary' being calculated by hanging chains].

Heartier, more care-free enjoyment of life I have never found in any creature.

The life of this comic redlegs, the mountain's merriest child, [possibly the American grasshopper: Schistocerca Americana]. seems to be made up of pure, condensed gaiety. The Douglas squirrel is the only living creature that I can compare him with in irrepressible jollity. Wonderful that these sublime mountains are so loudly cheered by a creature so queer. Nature in him seems to be snapping her fingers in the face of all earthly dejection. How the sound is made I do not understand. When he was on the ground he made not the slightest noise, nor when he was simply flying from place to place, but only when diving in curves, the motion seeming to be required for the sound; for the more vigorous the diving the more energetic the outbursts of jolly rattling.

I tried to observe him closely while he was resting between performances; but he would not allow me close, getting ready to spring for immediate flight, and keeping his eye on me. A fine sermon the little fellow danced for me on the Dome, a likely place to look for sermons in stones, but not for grasshopper sermons. A large and imposing pulpit for so small a preacher. No danger of weakness in the knees of the world while Nature can spring such a rattle as this. Even the bear did not express for me the mountain's happiness so tellingly as did this comical little hopper. No cloud of care in his day, no winter of discontent [Shakespearean ref: Richard 3rd: 'the winter of our discontent'] in sight. To him every day is a holiday; when at length his sun sets, I fancy he will cuddle down on the forest floor and die like the leaves and flowers, and like them leave no unsightly remains needing burial.

Sundown, and I must to camp. Good-night, friends three—brown bear, rugged boulder of energy in Eden-like gardens; restless, fussy fly with gauzy wings stirring the air all round the world; and grasshopper, crisp, spark of joy enlivening the massy sublimity of the mountains like the laugh of a child. Thank you, thank you all three for your quickening company. Heaven guide every wing and leg. Good-night friends three, good-night.

July 22. A fine specimen of the black-tailed deer went bounding past camp this morning. A buck with wide spread of antlers, showing admirable vigor and grace. Wonderful the beauty, strength, and graceful movements of wilderness animals, cared for by Nature, when our experience with domestic animals would lead us to fear that wild beasts would degenerate. Yet the upshot of Nature's method of breeding and teaching seems to lead to excellence of every sort. Deer, like all wild animals, are as clean as plants. Their beauty, alert or in repose, surprise yet more than their bounding strength. Every posture is graceful, the very poetry of manners and motion. Mother Nature is too often spoken of as in reality no mother at all. Yet how sternly, tenderly she looks after her children in all sorts of weather and wilderness.

The more I see of deer the more I admire them as mountaineers. They make their way into the heart of the roughest solitudes with smooth reserve of strength, through dense brush and forest encumbered with boulders and fallen trees, across canyons, roaring streams and snow-fields, ever showing forth beauty and courage. Over nearly all the continent the deer find homes. In the Florida savannas, in the Canadian woods, in the far north's mossy tundras, swimming lakes and rivers and arms of the sea from island to island washed with waves, or climbing rocky mountains, everywhere healthy, adding beauty to every landscape—a truly admirable creature and great credit to Nature.

Have been sketching a silver fir that stands on a ridge eastward of camp—a fine tree with a particular snow-storm story to tell. About one hundred feet high, growing on rock and rooting into a weathered joint less than an inch wide, its base bulging out to bear its weight. When young, a northerly storm broke it nearly to the ground, as is shown by the dead top leaning out from the living trunk, built up from a new shoot below the break. The annual rings that have overgrown the dead sapling tell the year of the storm. Wonderful that a side branch forming a portion of one of the level collars that encircle the trunk of this species (*Abies magnifica*) should grow erect and take the place of the lost axis to form a new tree.

Many others bear testimony to the crushing severity of this particular storm. Some, seventy-five feet high, were buried like grass, whole groves vanishing as if the forest had been cleared away, leaving nothing visible till the spring thaw. Then the best undamaged saplings rose again, aided by the wind, some reaching a nearly erect attitude, others remaining bent, while those with broken backs endeavored to specialize a side branch below the break to form a new axis of development. It is as if a bent-over man, his back broken, would find a branch backbone sprouting from below the break and gradually develop new arms, shoulders and head, while the old damaged parts died.

Grand white cloud mountains and domes created about noon as usual, ranges of endless variety, as if Nature loved this sort of work, doing it nearly every day with infinite industry, and producing beauty that never palls. A few zig-zags of lightning, five minutes' shower, then a gradual clearing.

July 23. Another midday cloudland, displaying power and beauty, but hopelessly unsketchable and untellable. What can poor mortals say: as a description of their glowing domes and ridges, shadowy gulfs and canyons, and feather-edged ravines is being tried, they vanish, leaving no visible ruins. Nevertheless, these fleeting sky mountains are as substantial as the more lasting upheavals of granite beneath them. Both are built up and die, and in God's calendar difference of duration is nothing. We can only dream about them with worshiping admiration, happier than we dare tell even to sympathetic friends, glad to know that not a crystal or vapor particle of them is lost; that they sink and vanish only to rise again in higher and higher beauty. As to our own work, duty, influence, etc, which we so fuss about, it will not fail of its due effect, though, like a lichen on a stone, we keep silent.

July 24. Noonday clouds occupying about half the sky gave half an hour of heavy rain to wash one of the cleanest landscapes in the world. How well it is washed! The sea is hardly less dusty than the ice-burnished pavements and ridges, domes and canyons, and summit peaks plashed with snow like waves with foam. How fresh the woods are and calm after the last film of cloud is wiped from the sky! A few minutes ago every tree was bowing to the roaring storm, tossing their branches in glorious enthusiasm like worship. But though to the ear these trees are now silent, their songs never cease. Every hidden cell is throbbing with music and life, every fibre thrilling like harp strings, while incense is ever flowing from the balsam bells and leaves. No wonder the hills and groves were God's first temples, and the more they are cut down and hewn into cathedrals and churches, the farther off and dimmer seems the Lord himself!

The same may be said of stone temples. To the east of our grove stands one of Nature's cathedrals, hewn from the living rock, almost conventional in form, about two thousand feet high, nobly adorned with spires and pinnacles, thrilling under floods of sunshine as if alive, and well named "Cathedral Peak." Even Shepherd Billy turns at times to this wonderful mountain building, though apparently deaf to all stone sermons. I have been trying to get him to walk to the brink of Yosemite for a view, offering to watch the sheep for a day. Within a mile of the famous valley, he will not go to it. "What," says he, "is Yosemite but a canyon—a lot of rocks—a hole in the ground—a place dangerous about falling into—a damned good place to keep away from." "But think of the waterfalls, Billy—just think of that big stream we crossed the other day, falling half a mile through the air—think of that, and the sound it makes. You can hear it now like the roar of the sea."

Thus I pressed Yosemite upon him like a missionary offering the gospel, but he would have none of it. "I should be afraid to look over so high a wall," he said. "It would make my head swim. There is nothing worth seeing anywhere, only rocks, and I see plenty of them here. Tourists that spend their money to see rocks and falls are fools, that's all. You can't humbug me. I've been in this country too long for that." Such souls, I suppose, are asleep, or befogged beneath mean pleasures and cares.

July 25. Another cloudland. Some clouds have an over-ripe look, watery and bedraggled and drawn out into shreds and patches, giving the sky a littered appearance; not so these clear, Sierra summer midday clouds. All are beautiful with smooth definite curves like those of glacier-polished domes. They begin to grow about eleven o'clock, and seem so wonderfully near from this high camp one is tempted to climb them and trace the streams that pour like cataracts from their shadowy fountains. Their rain is often very heavy, a sort of waterfall as imposing as if pouring from rock mountains. Never in all my travels have I found anything more truly novel and interesting than these midday sky mountains, their fine tones, majestic visible growth, ever-changing scenery and general effects, though mostly indescribable. I often think of Shelley's cloud poem, "I sift the snow on the mountains below."

CHAPTER VI

MOUNT HOFFMAN AND LAKE TENAYA

July 26, 1869. Ramble to the summit of Mount Hoffman at eleven thousand feet high, the highest point in life's journey thus far. And what glorious landscapes are about me, new plants, new animals, new crystals, and multitudes of new mountains far higher than Hoffman, [description of mountain landcape], the pure blue bell-flower sky brooding them all—a glory day of admission into a new realm of wonders as if Nature had wooingly whispered, "Come higher." What questions I asked, and how little I know of all the vast show, so hopeful of some day knowing more, learning the meaning of these divine symbols crowded on this wondrous page.

Mount Hoffman is the highest part of a ridge or spur about fourteen miles from the axis of the main range, perhaps a remnant isolated by unequal denudation. The southern slopes shed their waters into Yosemite Valley by Tenaya and Dome Creeks, the northern in part into the Tuolumne River, but mostly into the Merced via Yosemite Creek. The rock is mostly granite, with small crests rising here and there in picturesque castellated red metamorphic slates. Both granite and slates are divided by joints, making them separable into blocks like the stones of artificial masonry, suggesting the Scripture "He hath builded the mountains." [possibly from Ps 87:1]. Great banks of snow and ice are piled in hollows on the cool steep north side forming the highest perennial sources of Yosemite Creek. The southern slopes are much more gradual. Narrow slot-like gorges extend across the summit at right angles, formed evidently by the erosion of less resisting beds. They are usually called "devil's slides," though they lie far above the region usually haunted by the devil; for though we read that he once climbed a very high mountain [Luke 4:5 'Then the devil led Jesus up to a high place and showed him all the nations'], he can't be much of a mountaineer, for his tracks are seldom seen above the timber-line.

The broad gray summit is desolate in general, wasted by ages of gnawing storms; but looking closely at the surface one finds it covered by millions of charming plants with so small they form no mass of color visible at a distance. Beds of azure daisies smile confidingly in moist hollows, and along the banks of small rills, with several species of eriogonum, silky-leaved ivesia, pentstemon, orthocarpus, and patches of *Primula suffruticosa*, a beautiful shrubby species. Here also I found bryanthus, a charming heathwort with purple flowers and dark green foliage, and three trees new to me—a hemlock and two pines.

The hemlock (*Tsuga Mertensiana*) is the most beautiful conifer I have ever seen [decription]. It is now in full bloom, and the flowers, together with thousands of last season's cones, display wonderful wealth of brown and purple and blue. Gladly I climbed the first tree I found to revel in its midst. How the touch of the flowers makes one's flesh tingle! [description of the flowers]. How wonderful that, with all its delicate feminine grace, exposed to the wildest blasts, this lovely tree has already endured the storms of centuries!

The two pines also are brave storm-enduring trees, the mountain pine (*Pinus monticola*) and the dwarf pine (*Pinus albicaulis*). [description of tree]. Only a few storm-beaten adventurers approach the summits. The dwarf or white-bark pine forms the timber-line, completely dwarfed - one may walk over the top of a bed of it as over snow-pressed chaparral.

How boundless the day seems in these storm-beaten sky gardens amid the vast congregation of onlooking mountains! Admirable that the more chilly and storm-chafed the mountains, the finer the glow on their faces and the finer their plants. The myriad flowers tingeing the mountain-top seem less to have grown out of the rough gravel of disintegration, but seem as visitors, a cloud of witnesses to Nature's love in what we in our ignorant unbelief call howling desert. The apparently dull and forbidding ground, besides being rich in plants, sparkles with crystals: mica, hornblende, quartz, tourmaline. The radiance in some places is fairly dazzling, rays of every color sparkling in glorious abundance, joining the plants in their brave beauty—every crystal, every flower a window opening into heaven, a mirror reflecting the Creator.

From garden to garden, ridge to ridge, I drifted enchanted, now on my knees gazing into the face of a daisy, now climbing among the purple and azure flowers of the hemlocks, now down into the treasuries of the snow, or gazing afar over domes and peaks, lakes and woods, and the billowy glaciated fields of the upper Tuolumne, and trying to sketch them. In the midst of such beauty, pierced with its rays, one's body is all one tingling palate. Who wouldn't be a mountaineer! Up here all the world's prizes seem nothing.

The largest of the visible glacier lakes, showing the finest shore scenery, is Tenaya, about a mile long, with Cathedral Peak dipping its feet into its southern headwaters, while northwards are many smooth rock-waves and domes. In the southern distance a multitude of snowy peaks, the fountainheads of rivers. Lake Hoffman shimmers beneath my feet, ringed with pines. To the north the basin of Yosemite Creek glitters with lakelets; but the eye is soon drawn away from these bright mirrors to revel in the glorious congregation of peaks on the axis of the range, in their robes of snow and light.

Carlo caught an unfortunate woodchuck running from a grassy spot to its boulder home—one of the hardiest of the mountain animals. I could not save him. After telling Carlo that he not kill anything, I caught sight of the curious pika, or little chief hare, which cuts large quantities of lupines and other plants and lays them to dry for hay, which it stores in underground barns to last through the winter. Coming upon these plants freshly cut and lying in handfuls here and there on the rocks has a startling effect: these little haymakers, endowed with brain stuff something like our own—God up here looking after them—how they widen our sympathy!

An eagle soaring above a cliff, where I suppose its nest is, makes another striking show of life, and brings to mind the other people of the so-called solitude—deer caring for their young; the strong, well-clad bears; the lively throng of squirrels; the blessed birds; and the clouds of happy insects filling the sky with joyous hum as part and parcel of the down-pouring sunshine. All these come to mind, as well as the plant-people and glad streams singing their way to the sea. But most impressive of all is the vast glowing countenance of the wilderness in awesome, infinite repose.

Toward sunset enjoyed a fine run to camp, down the long south slopes, across ridges and ravines, gardens and avalanche gaps, through the firs and chaparral, enjoying wild excitement and excess of strength, and so ends a day that will never end.

July 27. Up and away to Lake Tenaya—another big day, enough for a lifetime. The rocks, the air, everything speaking or silent; joyful, enchanting, banishing weariness and sense of time. No longing for anything now or hereafter as we go home into the mountain's heart. The level sunbeams are touching the fir-tops, every leaf shining with dew. Am heading east, the deep canyon of Tenaya Creek to my right, Mount Hoffman on the left, and the lake straight ahead about ten miles. Mount Hoffman is about three thousand feet above, Tenaya Creek four thousand feet below and separated from the shallow, irregular valley, (my way ahead), by smooth domes and wave-ridges. Many mossy emerald bogs and gardens in rocky hollows to go through—and what fine plants they give me, and how many views are displayed of the Hoffman and Cathedral Peak masonry, and what shining granite pavements to traverse about the shores of the lake!

On I sauntered in freedom complete; body without weight as far as I was aware; now wading through starry parnassia bogs, [list of species]; then down a broad, majestic stairway into the ice-sculptured lake-basin.

The snow is melting fast, and the streams are singing bank-full, swaying softly, quivering with sun-spangles, swirling in pot-holes, resting in pools, leaping, shouting in wild energy over boulder dams, joyful in every form. No Sierra landscape that I have seen holds anything truly dead or dull, or any trace of what in manufacture is called rubbish; everything is perfectly clean and full of divine lessons. This quick, inevitable interest attaching to everything seems marvelous until the hand of God becomes visible: what interests Him may well interest us. When we try to pick out anything by itself, we find it hitched to everything else in the universe. One fancies a heart like our own must be beating in every crystal and cell, and we feel like stopping to speak to the plants and animals as friendly fellow mountaineers. Nature as a poet, an enthusiastic workingman, becomes more and more visible the farther and higher we go; for the mountains are fountains—beginning places, however related to sources beyond mortal ken.

I found three kinds of meadows: (1) Those contained in basins not yet filled with earth enough to make a dry surface. They are planted with several species of carex, and have their margins diversified with robust flowering plants such as veratrum, larkspur, lupine, etc.

(2) Those contained in the same sort of basins, once lakes like the first, but so situated in relation to streams and beds of sand, gravel, etc., that they are now high and dry. This dry condition and corresponding difference in their vegetation may be caused simply by the basin being shallow and therefore sooner filled. They are planted with grasses, mostly fine, silky, and rather short-leaved, *Calamagrostis* and *Agrostis* being the principal genera. They form delightfully smooth, level sods in which one finds two or three species of gentian and as many of purple and yellow orthocarpus, violet, vaccinium, kalmia, bryanthus, and lonicera.

(3) Meadows hanging on ridges and mountain slopes, not in basins, but held up by masses of boulders and fallen trees, which, forming dams one above another in close succession on small streams, have collected soil enough for the growth of grasses, carices, and many flowering plants, being kept well-watered without currents strong enough to carry them away, a hanging meadow is the result. Their surfaces are roughened more or less by the projecting tops of the dam rocks or logs; but at a little distance this roughness is not noticed, and the effect is very striking—bright green, down-sweeping flowery ribbons on gray slopes.

The broad shallow streams these meadows belong to are mostly derived from banks of snow. Because the soil is well-drained in some places, while in others the dam rocks are packed close and caulked with bits of wood and leaves, making boggy patches; the vegetation is correspondingly varied. I saw patches of willow, bryanthus, and a fine show of lilies on some of them, not forming a margin, but scattered about among the carex and grass. Most of these meadows are now in their prime. How wonderful must be the temper of the elastic leaves of grasses and sedges to make curves so perfect. Tempered a little harder, they would stand erect like strips of metal; a little softer, and every leaf would lie flat. And what fine painting and tinting there is on the glumes and pales, stamens and feathery pistils. Butterflies colored like the flowers waver above them in wonderful profusion, and many other beautiful winged people, numbered and known and by the Lord, are waltzing together high over head, seemingly in hilarious enjoyment of their little sparks of life. How do they get a living, and endure the weather? How are their little bodies, with muscles, nerves, organs, kept in such admirable exuberant health? Regarded only as mechanical inventions, compared with these, Godlike man's greatest machines are as nothing.

Most of the sandy gardens on moraines are in prime beauty like the meadows, though some in cooler situations have not yet bloomed. On sunny sheets of crystalline soil along the slopes of the Hoffman Mountains, I saw extensive patches of ivesia and purple gilia with scarce a green leaf, making fine clouds of color. Ribes bushes, vaccinium, and kalmia, now in flower, make beautiful rugs and borders along the streams. Shaggy beds of dwarf oak (*Quercus chrysolepis*, var. *vaccinifolia*) over which one may walk are common on rocky moraines, yet this is the same species as the large live oak seen near Brown's Flat. The most beautiful of the shrubs is the purple-flowered bryanthus, here making glorious carpets at nine thousand feet.

The principal tree for the first mile or two from camp is the magnificent silver fir, which reaches perfection here both in size and form, and groups in groves with open spaces between. So trim and tasteful are these spiry groves one would fancy they must have been placed in position by some master gardener, their regularity seeming almost by convention. But Nature is the only gardener able to do work so fine. Centrally, a few noble specimens two hundred feet disperse younger trees around them; and outside of these another circle of yet smaller ones, the whole arranged like bouquets, every tree fitting nicely the place assigned to it; with small roses and eriogonums found blooming about the groves, forming charming pleasure grounds.

Higher, the firs shrink to a lesser perfection, many showing double summits, indicating storm stress. Still, where good moraine soil is found, even on the rim of the lake-basin, specimens one hundred and fifty feet in height and five feet in diameter occur at nearly nine thousand feet. The saplings are mostly bent with the crushing weight of the winter snow, which at this elevation must be at least eight or ten feet deep, enough bury young trees twenty or thirty feet in height and hold them down for four or five months. Some trees break; others spring up when the snow melts - at length attaining a size that enables them to withstand the snow. Yet even in trees five feet thick the traces of this early discipline are still plainly to be seen in their curved insteps; in old dried saplings protruding from the trunk, partially overgrown by the new axis developed from below the break. Yet through all this stress the forest is maintained in marvelous beauty.

Above the silver firs I find the two-leaved pine (*Pinus contorta*, var. *Murrayana*) forms the bulk of the forest to ten thousand feet or more—the highest timber-belt of the Sierra. I saw a specimen nearly five feet in diameter growing on deep, well-watered soil at an elevation of about nine thousand feet. The form of this species varies very much with position, exposure, soil, etc. Closely-grown on stream-banks it is very slender; some specimens seventy-five feet high do not exceed five inches in diameter at the ground. The average diameter when full grown at this elevation is about twelve or fourteen inches, height forty or fifty feet, the straggling branches bent up at the end, the bark thin and bedraggled with amber-colored resin. [Description of tree] ..sulphur-yellow flowers in showy clusters, giving a remarkably rich effect—a brave, hardy mountaineer pine, growing cheerily on rough areas as well as in fertile hollows, up to the waist in snow for centuries, facing a thousand storms and blooming every year in colors as bright as those worn by sun-drenched trees of the tropics.

A still hardier mountaineer is the Sierra juniper (*Juniperus occidentalis*), growing mostly on domes and ridges and glacier pavements. A sturdy highlander, content to live for more than a score of centuries on sunshine and snow; dogged endurance expressed in every feature, lasting about as long as the granite he stands on. Some are nearly as broad as high. I saw one on the shore of the lake nearly ten feet in diameter, and many six to eight feet. The bark, cinnamon-colored, flakes off in long ribbon-like strips with a satiny luster. It never seems to die a natural death, or even to fall after it has been killed. If protected from accidents, it would perhaps be immortal. I saw some that had withstood an avalanche from Mount Hoffman cheerily putting out new branches, as if repeating, like Grip, "Never say die." [Grip was a character in Charles Dickens's 'Barnaby Rudge' – the saying itself has been in English since the mid-1800's]. Some were simply standing on the pavement where no fissure more than half an inch wide offered a hold for its roots. The common height for these rock-dwellers is ten to twenty feet; most of the old ones have broken tops and are mere stumps with a few tufted branches: brown pillars on bare pavements, with elbow-room aplenty and clear views in every direction. On good moraine soil it reaches a height of forty to sixty feet, with dense gray foliage. The rings of the trunk are very thin, eighty to an inch. Those ten feet in diameter must be very old—many thousands of years.

Wish I could live, like them, on sunshine and snow, and stand with them by Lake Tenaya for a thousand years. How much I should see, and how delightful it would be! Everything in the mountains would find me and come to me, and everything from the heavens like light.

The lake was named for one of the chiefs of the Yosemite tribe. Old Tenaya is said to have been a good Indian to his tribe. When soldiers followed his band into Yosemite to punish them for cattle-stealing and other crimes, they fled to this lake early in spring through deep snow by a trail that leads out of the upper end of the valley, but being pursued, they lost heart and surrendered. A fine monument the old man has in this bright lake, though lakes die as well as Indians, being gradually filled with detritus carried in by the feeding streams, avalanches, rain and wind. Much of the Tenaya basin is already changed into a forested flat and meadow at the upper end, where the main tributary enters from Cathedral Peak. Two other tributaries come from the Hoffman Range. The outlet flows west through Tenaya Canyon to join the Merced River in Yosemite.

Scarce a handful of loose soil is to be seen on the north shore. All is bare, shining granite, suggesting the Indian name of the lake, Pywiack, meaning shining rock. The basin has been slowly excavated by the ancient glaciers, a work requiring countless millenia. On the south side an imposing mountain rises from the water's edge to a height of around three thousand feet, feathered with hemlock and pine; and huge shining domes on the east, over the tops of which the grinding, wasting, molding glacier must have swept as the wind does today.

July 28. No cloud mountains, only curly cirrus wisps scarce perceptible, and the want of thunder to strike the noon hour seems strange, as if the Sierra clock had stopped. Have been studying the *magnifica* fir—measured one near two hundred and forty feet high, the tallest I have yet seen. This species is the most symmetrical of all conifers, but though gigantic in size it seldom lives more than four or five hundred years. Most of the trees die from the attacks of a fungus at the age of two or three centuries. This dry-rot fungus perhaps enters the trunk by way of the stumps of limbs broken off by the snow that loads the broad, palmate branches.

The younger specimens are marvels of symmetry, straight and erect as a plumb-line, their branches in level whorls of five mostly, each branch as exact in its divisions as a fern frond, and thickly covered by the leaves, making a rich plush over all the tree excepting the trunk and a small portion of the main limbs. The up-turned leaves are stiff and sharp, pointed on the upper portion of the tree. They remain on the tree about eight or ten years, and as the growth is rapid it is not rare to find leaves still in place on the upper axis where it is three to four inches in diameter, wide apart of course, their spiral arrangement beautifully displayed. The leaf-scars are conspicuous for twenty years or more, but there is a good deal of variation in different trees as to the thickness and sharpness of the leaves.

After the excursion to Mount Hoffman I had seen a complete cross-section of the Sierra forest, and I find that *Abies magnifica* is the most symmetrical tree of all the noble coniferous company. The cones are superb in form, size, and color, cylindrical, stand erect on the upper branches like casks, and are from five to eight inches in length by three or four in diameter, greenish gray, and covered with fine down which has a silvery luster in the sunshine, and their brilliance is augmented by beads of transparent balsam which seems to have been poured over each cone, bringing to mind the old

[Biblical] ceremonies of anointing with oil. If possible, the inside of the cone is more beautiful than the outside; the scales, bracts, and seed wings are tinted with the loveliest rosy purple with lustrous iridescence; the seeds, three fourths of an inch long, are dark brown.

When the cones are ripe the scales and bracts fall off, setting the seeds free to fly to their predestined places, while the dead spike-like axes are left on the branches for years to mark the positions of the vanished cones, excepting those cut off when green by the Douglas squirrel. How he gets his teeth under the broad bases of the sessile cones, I don't know. Climbing these trees on a sunny day to visit the growing cones and to gaze over the tops of the forest is one of my best enjoyments.

July 29. Bright, cool, exhilarating. Clouds about .05. Another glorious day of rambling, sketching, and universal enjoyment.

July 30. Clouds .20, but the regular shower did not reach us, though thunder was heard a few miles off, striking the noon hour. Ants, flies, and mosquitoes enjoy this fine climate. A few houseflies have discovered our camp. The Sierra mosquitoes are courageous and of good size, some of them measuring nearly an inch from tip of sting to tip of folded wings. Though less abundant than in most wildernesses, they occasionally make quite a hum and stir, and pay but little attention to time or place. They sting anywhere, anytime, wherever they find anything worthwhile, until they are themselves stung by frost. The large, jet-black ants are only ticklish and troublesome when one is lying down under the trees.

Noticed a borer drilling a silver fir. Ovipositor about an inch and a half in length, polished and straight like a needle. When not in use, it is folded back in a sheath, which extends straight behind like the legs of a crane in flying. This drilling, I suppose, is to save nest building, and the aftercare of feeding the young. Who would guess that in the brain of a fly so much knowledge could find lodgement? How do they know that their eggs will hatch in such holes, or, after they hatch, that the soft, helpless grubs will find the right sort of nourishment in silver fir sap?

This domestic arrangement calls to mind the curious family of gallflies. Each species knows what kind of plant will respond to the stimulus of the puncture it makes and the eggs it lays, in forming a growth that not only provides a home but also provides food for the young. Probably these gallflies make mistakes at times, like anybody else; but when they do, there is simply a failure of that particular brood, while enough to perpetuate the species do find the proper plants and nourishment. Many mistakes of this kind might be made without being discovered by us. Once a pair of wrens built a nest in the sleeve of a workman's coat, which was called for at sundown, much to the consternation of the birds.

Still, the marvel remains that any of the children of such small people as gnats and mosquitoes should escape their own and their parents' mistakes, as well as the vicissitudes of the weather and hosts of enemies, and come forth in full vigor and perfection to enjoy the sunny world. When we think of the small creatures that are visible, we are led to think of many that are smaller still and lead us on and on into infinite mystery. [In this paragraph Muir comes close to the theory of natural selection – the point he misses is that the parents who 'make mistakes' do not get to pass on as many children!].

July 31. Another glorious day, the air as delicious to the lungs as nectar to the tongue, indeed, the body seems one palate, and tingles equally throughout. Cloudiness about .05, but our ordinary shower has not yet reached us, though I hear distant thunder.

The cheery little chipmunk, so common about Brown's Flat, is common here also, and perhaps other species. In their light, airy habits they recall the familiar species of the Eastern States, which we admired in the oak openings of Wisconsin as they skimmed along the zigzag rail fences. These Sierra chipmunks are more arboreal and squirrel-like. I first noticed them on the lower edge of the coniferous belt, where the Sabine and yellow pines meet—exceedingly interesting little fellows, full of odd ways, and without being true squirrels have most of their accomplishments without their quarrelsomeness. I never weary of watching them frisking about the bushes gathering seeds and berries, like song sparrows poising daintily on slender twigs, and making even less stir than most birds of the same size.

Few of the Sierra animals interest me more; they are so able, confiding and beautiful, they take one's heart. Though weighing hardly more than field mice, they are laborious collectors and therefore well fed, but never in the least bloated. On the contrary, of their frisky liveliness there is no end. They have a variety of notes corresponding with their movements, some sweet and liquid, like water tinkling into pools. They seem to love teasing dogs, coming frequently almost within reach, then frisking away with lively chipping like sparrows, beating time to their music with their tails, which at each chip describe half circles from side to side. Not even the Douglas squirrel is surer-footed or more fearless. I have seen them running about on sheer precipices of the Yosemite walls seemingly holding on with as little effort as flies, and as unconscious of danger, where, if the slightest slip were made, they would have fallen two or three thousand feet. How fine it would be could we mountaineers climb these tremendous cliffs with the same grip! The venture I made the other day for a view of the Yosemite Fall, and which tried my nerves so sorely, this little Tamias [chipmunk] would have made for an ear of grass.

The woodchuck (*Arctomys monax*) of the bleak mountain-tops is a very different sort of mountaineer—the most bovine of rodents, a heavy eater, fat, aldermanic in bulk in his high pastures, like a cow in a clover field. One woodchuck would outweigh a hundred chipmunks, and yet he is by no means a dull animal. In the midst of what we regard as storm-beaten desolation he pipes and whistles right cheerily, and enjoys long life in his skyland homes. His burrow is made in disintegrated rocks or beneath large boulders. Coming out of his den in frosty mornings, he sunbathes on some flat-topped rock, then breakfasts in garden hollows on grass and flowers till comfortably swollen, then goes a-visiting to fight and play. How long a woodchuck lives in this bracing air I don't know, but some of them are rusty and gray like lichen-covered boulders.

August 1. A grand cloudland and five-minute shower, refreshing the blessed wilderness, already so fragrant and fresh, steeping the black meadow mold and dead leaves like tea.

The waycup, or flicker, so familiar to every boy in the Mid-West, is one of the most common wood-peckers here, and makes one feel at home. I see no difference in plumage or habits from the Eastern species, though the climate here is so different—a fine, brave, confiding bird. The robin, too, is here, with all his familiar notes and gestures, tripping daintily on open gardens and high meadows. Over all America he seems to be at home, plains to mountains and north to south, with the march of the seasons and food supply. How admirable the constitution of this brave singer, keeping in cheery health over so varied a range! Often, as I wander through these solemn woods, awe-struck and silent, I hear the reassuring voice of this fellow wanderer ringing sweet and clear, "Fear not! fear not!"

The mountain quail (*Oreortyx ricta*) I often meet in my walks—a small brown partridge with a slender, ornamental crest worn jauntily like a feather in a boy's cap, giving it a very marked appearance. This species is considerably larger than the valley quail common on the hot foothills. They seldom alight in trees, but love to wander in flocks of from five to twenty through the ceanothus and manzanita thickets and over open meadows and rocks where the forest is less dense, uttering a low cluck to keep them all together. When disturbed they rise with a strong birr of wing-beats, and scatter as if exploded to a distance of a quarter of a mile or so. After the danger is past they call one another together with a loud piping note— Nature's beautiful mountain chickens.

I have not yet found their nests. The young of this season are already hatched and away—new wanderers half as large as their parents. I wonder how they live through the long winters, when the ground is ten foot in snow. They must go towards the lower edge of the forest, like the deer, though I have not heard of them there.

The blue, or dusky grouse is also common here. They like the densest fir woods, and when disturbed, burst from the branches of the trees with a strong, loud whir, then vanish in a wavering, silent slide, without moving a feather—a stout, beautiful bird about the size of the prairie chicken, spending most of the time in the trees, excepting the breeding season, when it keeps to the ground. The young are now able to fly. When scattered by man or dog, they keep still until danger is passed, then the mother calls them together. The chicks can hear the call a distance of several hundred yards, though it is not loud. Should the young be unable to fly, the mother feigns desperate lameness to draw one away, throwing herself at one's feet within two or three yards, rolling over on her back, kicking and gasping, so as to deceive man or beast.

They are said to stay all the year in the woods, taking shelter in dense branches of fir and yellow pine during snowstorms, and feeding on the young buds. Their legs are feathered to the toes, and I have never heard of their suffering in any sort of weather. Able to live on pine buds, they are independent in the matter of food, which troubles so many of us. I would gladly live forever on pine buds, however full of turpentine, for the sake of this grand independence. Just to think of our sufferings last month merely for grist-mill flour! Man seems to have more difficulty in gaining food than any other of the Lord's creatures. For many in towns it is a lifelong struggle; for others, the danger of coming to want is so great, the deadly habit of endless hoarding forms, which smothers all real life and is continued long after every reasonable need has been over-supplied.

On Mount Hoffman I saw a curious dove-colored bird that seemed half woodpecker, half crow. It screams something like a crow, but flies like a woodpecker, and has a long, straight bill, with which I saw it opening pinecones. It seems to keep to the heights, though no doubt it comes down for shelter during winter, if not for food. These bird-mountaineers, I guess, can glean nuts enough, even in winter, from the different kinds of conifers; for always a few nuts remain in the cones for hungry winter gleaners.

CHAPTER VII

A STRANGE EXPERIENCE

August 2, 1869. Clouds and showers, about the same as yesterday. Sketching all day on the North Dome until about five o'clock in the afternoon, when, as I was thinking only of the glorious Yosemite landscape, trying to draw every tree and every line and feature of the rocks, I was suddenly possessed with the notion that my friend, Professor J. D. Butler, of the University of Wisconsin, was below me in the valley, and I jumped up with almost as much excitement as if he had suddenly touched me. Leaving my work without the slightest deliberation, I ran down the western slope of the Dome and along the valley wall, looking for a way down, till until I came to a vegetated side canyon, which I thought might afford a practical way into the valley, and immediately began to make the descent.

After a little, common sense told me that it would be long after dark before I could possibly reach the hotel, that the visitors would be asleep, that nobody would know me, that I had no money in my pockets, and moreover was without a coat. I therefore stopped, and finally succeeded in reasoning myself out of the notion of seeking my friend in the dark, whose presence I only felt in a strange, telepathic way. I dragged myself back through the woods to camp, never for a moment wavering, however, in my determination to go down to him next morning.

This is the most unexplainable notion that ever struck me. Had some one whispered in my ear while I sat on the Dome, that Professor Butler was in the valley, I could not have been more surprised.

When I was leaving the university, he said, "Now, John, I want to hold you in sight and watch your career. Promise to write me at least once a year." I had a letter from him in July, at our first camp in the Hollow, dated May, saying he might possibly visit this summer, and therefore hoped to meet me. But as he named no meeting-place, and gave no directions as to his itinerary, and as I should be in the wilderness all summer, I had not the slightest hope of seeing him. Thus had the matter vanished from my mind until this afternoon, when he seemed to be wafted bodily almost against my face. Well, to-morrow I shall see.

August 3. Had a wonderful day. Found Professor Butler as the compass-needle finds the pole. So last evening's telepathy, or whatever it was, was true; for he had just entered the valley by the Coulterville Trail and was coming up the valley past El Capitan when his presence struck me. Had he looked to the North Dome with a good glass when it first came in sight, he might have seen me jump up and run toward him. This seems the one well-defined supernatural event of my life; for, absorbed in Nature, spirit-rappings, second sight, ghost stories, etc., have never interested me since boyhood, seeming far less wonderful than Nature's open beauty.

This morning I was troubled because I had no suitable clothes, and at best am desperately shy. I was determined to go, however, to see my old friend after two years among strangers; got on a clean pair of overalls, a cashmere shirt, and a sort of jacket—the best my camp wardrobe afforded—tied my notebook on my belt, and strode away on my strange journey, followed by Carlo. I made my way though the gap discovered last evening, which proved to be Indian Canyon. There was no trail in it, and the rocks and brush were so rough that

Carlo frequently called me back to help him down precipitous places. Emerging from the canyon shadows, I found a man making hay, and asked him whether Professor Butler was in the valley. "I don't know," he replied; "but you can easily find out at the hotel."

In front of the gloomy hotel I found a tourist party adjusting their fishing tackle. They stared at me as if I had dropped from the clouds, mostly, I suppose, on account of my garb. I was told the office was locked, and that the landlord was away, but I might find the landlady, Mrs. Hutchings, in the parlor. I entered in a sad state of embarrassment, and after I had waited in the empty room and knocked at several doors she at length appeared, and said she rather thought Professor Butler *was* in the valley, but to make sure, she would bring the register from the office. Among the names I soon discovered the Professor's familiar handwriting, at the sight of which bashfulness vanished; and having learned that his party had gone up the valley, probably to the Vernal and Nevada Falls, I pushed on in glad pursuit.

In less than an hour I reached the head of the Nevada Canyon at the Vernal Fall, and just outside of the spray discovered a distinguished-looking gentleman, who regarded me curiously. When I made bold to inquire if he knew where Professor Butler was, instead of answering my question, he asked with military sharpness, "Who wants him?" "I want him," I replied with equal sharpness. "Why? Do *you* know him?" "Yes," I said. "Do *you* know him?"

Astonished that anyone in the mountains could possibly know Professor Butler and find him in the valley, he came down to me and courteously replied, "Yes, I know Professor Butler very well. I am General Alvord, and we were fellow students in Rutland, Vermont, long ago, when we were both young." "But where is he now?" I persisted, cutting short his story. "He has gone beyond the falls with a companion, to try to climb that big rock, the top of which you can see." His guide now volunteered the information that it was the Liberty Cap, and that if I waited at the head of the fall I should be sure to find them on their way down. I climbed the ladders by the Vernal Fall, determined to go to the top of Liberty Cap rock in my hurry. So heart-hungry at times may one be to see a friend in the flesh, however carefree one's life may be. Just above the brow of the Vernal Fall I caught sight of him in the brush and rocks, half erect, groping along, evidently very hot and tired.

When he saw me he sat down on a boulder to wipe the perspiration from his brow, and taking me for one of the guides, asked the way to the fall ladders. I pointed out the path marked with little piles of stones. He called his companion. I said, "Professor Butler, don't you know me?" "I think not," he replied; but sudden recognition followed, and astonishment that I should have found him. "John Muir, John Muir, where have you come from?" I told him the story of my feeling his presence when he entered the valley last evening, when he was four or five miles distant. This, of course, only made him wonder the more.

Below the foot of the Vernal Fall the guide was waiting with his saddle-horse, and I walked along the trail, chatting all the way back to the hotel, talking of school days, friends in Madison, of the students, how each had prospered, etc., gazing at the stupendous rocks about us, now growing indistinct in the gloaming, and again quoting from the poets—a rare ramble. It was late when we reached the hotel, and General Alvord was waiting. When I was introduced he seemed yet more astonished than the Professor at my descent from cloudland and going straight to my friend. They had come direct from the East, had not yet visited any of their friends in the state, and considered themselves undiscoverable.

At dinner, the General leaned back in his chair, and looking down the table, thus introduced me to the dozen guests or so: "This man, you know, came down out of these huge, trackless mountains, you know, to find his friend Professor Butler here, the very day he arrived; and how did he know he was here? He just felt him, he says. This is the queerest case of Scotch farsightedness I ever heard of," etc. While my friend quoted Shakespeare: "More things in heaven and earth, Horatio, than are dreamt of in your philosophy," "As the sun, ere he has risen, sometimes paints his image in the firmament, even so the shadows of events precede the events, and in today already walks to-morrow."

After dinner we talked of Madison days. The Professor wants me to go with him on a camping trip in the Hawaiian Islands; I tried to get him to camp with me in the high Sierra. But he says, "Not now." He must not leave the General. I was surprised to learn they will leave the valley tomorrow or next day. I'm glad I'm not great enough to be missed in the busy world.

August 4. Strange to sleep in a paltry hotel chamber after the spacious luxury of the starry sky and silver firs. Bade farewell to my friend and the General. The kind old soldier was very kind. He told me long stories of the Florida Seminole war, in which he took part, and invited me to visit him in Omaha. Calling Carlo, I scrambled home through the Indian Canyon gate, pitying the poor Professor and General, bound by clocks, duties, etc., and compelled to dwell with lowland care, dust and din, where Nature is covered and her voice smothered, while the poor, insignificant wanderer enjoys the freedom of God's wilderness.

Apart from the human interest of my visit today, I greatly enjoyed Yosemite, which I had visited only once before, having spent eight days last spring in rambling amid its rocks and waters. Wherever we go in the mountains, or indeed in any of God's wild fields, we find more than we seek. Descending four thousand feet in a few hours, we enter a new world—climate, plants, sounds, inhabitants, and scenery all changed. Near camp the goldcup oak forms sheets of chaparral, on top of which we may make our beds. Going down the Indian Canyon we observe this little bush changing by regular gradations to a large bush, to a small tree, and then larger, until on the rocky taluses [Latin: talus = ankle, the heaps of boulders fallen off cliffs] near the bottom of the valley we find it developed into a broad, picturesque tree from four to eight feet in diameter, and forty or fifty feet high. Innumerable too are the forms of water displayed: each gliding reach, cascade, and fall has its own character.

Had a good view of the Vernal and Nevada, two of the main falls of the valley, less than a mile apart, and offering striking differences. The Vernal, four hundred feet high and about seventy-five or eighty feet wide, drops smoothly over a round-lipped precipice and forms a superb apron of slightly fluted embroidery, green and white, maintaining this form nearly to the bottom, where it is suddenly veiled in quick-flying billows of spray and mist, in which the afternoon sunbeams play with ravishing rainbow colors.

The Nevada is white from its first appearance as it leaps out into the freedom of the air. At its head it presents a twisted appearance, by an overfolding of the current from striking the side of its channel just before its first out-bounding leap. About two thirds of the way down, the hurrying throng of comet-shaped masses glance on an inclined part of the precipice and are beaten into yet whiter foam, greatly expanded, and sent bounding outward, making an indescribably glorious show, especially when the afternoon sunshine is pouring into it. In this fall—one of the most wonderful in the world—the water does not seem to be under the dominion of ordinary laws, but rather as if it were a living creature, full of the strength of the mountains and their huge, wild joy.

From beneath heavy throbbing blasts of spray the broken river is seen emerging in ragged boulder-chafed strips. These are speedily gathered into a roaring torrent. On it goes, shouting, roaring, exulting in its strength, passes through a gorge with sublime energy, then suddenly expands on a gently inclined pavement, rushing down in thin sheets and folds of lace-work into a quiet pool—"Emerald Pool," as it is called—a period separating two grand sentences. Resting here long enough to part with its foam-bells and gray mixtures of air, it glides quietly to the verge of the Vernal precipice in a broad sheet. A new display in the Vernal Fall; then more rapids and rock tossings down the canyon, shaded by live oak, Douglas spruce, fir, maple, and dogwood. It receives the Illilouette tributary, and sweeps out into the sun-filled valley to join the other streams which, like itself, have danced and sung their way down from snowy heights to form the main Merced—the river of Mercy. But of this there is no end, and life, when one thinks of it, is so short. Never mind, one day in the midst of these divine glories is well worth toiling and starving for.

Professor Butler he gave me a book, and I gave him one of my pencil sketches for his little son Henry, a favorite of mine. He made many visits to my room when I was a student. Never shall I forget his patriotic speeches for the Union, mounted on a tall stool, when he was only six years old.

Strange that visitors to Yosemite seem so little influenced by its novel grandeur, as if with eyes bandaged and ears stopped they look down as if wholly unconscious of their surroundings, while the sublime rocks were trembling with the tones of the mighty chanting congregation of waters gathered from the mountains round about, making music that might draw angels out of heaven. [Possibly Muir is being a little unfair – these visitors may just have been stunned by the beauty around them].

Yet respectable, even wise-looking people were fixing bits of worms on bent pieces of wire to catch trout. Sport they called it. Should church-goers pass the time fishing in baptismal fonts while dull sermons were being preached, the so-called sport might not be so bad; but to play in the Yosemite temple, seeking pleasure in the pain of fishes struggling for their lives, while God himself is preaching his sublimest water and stone sermons!

Now I'm back at the camp-fire, and can't help thinking about my psychic recognition of my friend's presence. It seems supernatural, but only because it is not understood. But silly to make so much of it while the natural is more truly marvelous and mysterious than the so-called supernatural. Most of the miracles we hear of are infinitely less wonderful than the commonest natural phenomena. Perhaps the invisible rays that struck me while I sat working on the Dome are like those which attract and repel people at first sight, concerning which much nonsense has been written. The worst effect of these odd things is blindness to the divinely common. Hawthorne, I fancy, could weave one of his weird romances out of this little telepathic episode, probably replacing my good old Professor by an attractive woman.

August 5. We were awakened this morning before daybreak by the furious barking of Carlo and Jack and the sound of stampeding sheep. Billy fled from his punk bed to the fire, and refused to stir into the darkness to try to gather the scattered flock, or find the nature of the disturbance. It was a bear attack, as we afterward learned, and I suppose little was gained by trying to do anything before daylight. Nevertheless, being anxious to know what was up, Carlo and I groped our way through the woods, guided by the rustling sound made by fragments of the flock, not fearing the bear, for I knew that the runaways would go from their enemy as far as possible and Carlo's nose was also dependable.

About half a mile east of the corral we overtook twenty or thirty of the flock and succeeded in driving them back; then turning west, we traced another band of fugitives and got them back. After daybreak I found the remains of half a sheep carcass, still warm, showing that Bruin must have been enjoying his early mutton breakfast while I was seeking the runaways. Six dead sheep lay in the corral, smothered by the piling up of the flock against the side of the corral wall when the bear entered. Making a wide circuit of the camp, Carlo and I discovered a third band of fugitives and drove them back to camp. We also discovered another dead sheep half-eaten, showing there had been two of the shaggy freebooters at this early breakfast. They were easily traced. They had each caught a sheep, jumped over the corral fence with them, carrying them as a cat carries a mouse, laid them at the foot of fir trees a hundred yards or so back from the corral, and eaten their fill.

After breakfast I set out to seek more of the lost, and found seventy-five a considerable distance from camp. In the afternoon I succeeded, with Carlo's help, in getting them back to the flock. I don't know whether all are together again or not. I shall make a big fire this evening and keep watch.

When I asked Billy why he made his bed against the corral in rotten wood, when so many better places offered, he replied that he "wished to be as near the sheep as possible in case bears should attack them." Now that the bears have come, he has moved his bed to the far side of the camp, and seems afraid that he may be mistaken for a sheep.

This has been mostly a sheep day, and of course studies have been interrupted. Nevertheless, the walk through the gloom of the woods before dawn was worthwhile, and I have learned something about these noble bears. Their tracks are very telling, and so are their breakfasts.

Scarce a trace of clouds today, and of course our ordinary midday thunder is wanting.

August 6. Enjoyed the grand illumination of the camp grove, last night, from the fire we made to frighten the bears—compensation for loss of sleep and sheep. The noble pillars of verdure, vividly aglow, seemed to shoot into the sky like the flames that lighted them. Nevertheless, one of the bears paid us another visit, as if more attracted than repelled by the fire, climbed into the corral, killed a sheep and made off with it without being seen, while still another sheep was lost by trampling against the side of the corral. Now that our mutton has been tasted, I suppose it will be difficult to stop the ravages of these freebooters.

The Don arrived today from the lowlands with provisions and a letter. On learning the losses he had sustained, he determined to move the flock at once to the Upper Tuolumne region, saying that the bears would visit the camp every night as long as we stayed, and that no fire or noise we might make would frighten them.

No clouds save a few thin, lustrous touches on the eastern horizon. Thunder heard in the distance.

A glacier makes its way from the high peaks.

CHAPTER VIII

THE MONO TRAIL

August 7, 1869. Early this morning bade good-bye to the bears and blessed silver fir camp, and moved slowly east along the Mono Trail. At sundown camped for the night on one of the many small flowery meadows so greatly enjoyed on my Lake Tenaya excursion. The dusty, noisy flock seems outrageously foreign in these nature gardens, more so than bears among sheep. The harm they do goes to the heart, but glorious hope above the dust and din bids me look forward to a good time when money earned will enable me to go walking in pure wildness, with what I can carry on my back, and when the bread-sack is empty, run down to the bread-line for more. Nor will these run-downs be blanks, for, whether up or down, every step and jump on these blessed mountains is full of fine lessons.

August 8. Camp at the west end of Lake Tenaya. Arriving early, I took a walk on the glacier-polished pavements along the north shore, and climbed the magnificent shining mountain rock at the east end. Almost every yard shows the scoring and polishing of a great glacier that swept heavily over its summit, though it is about two thousand feet above the lake and ten thousand above sea-level. This majestic ice-flood came from the east, as the scoring shows. Even under water, the rock in some places is still grooved and polished; the waves have not yet obliterated even the superficial marks of glaciation. In climbing the steepest polished places I had to take off shoes and stockings.

A fine region this for study of glacial action in mountain-making. I found many charming plants: arctic daisies, phlox, white spiræa, bryanthus, and rock-ferns—pellæa, cheilanthes, allosorus—fringing weathered seams all the way up to the summit; and sturdy junipers, grand old gray and brown monuments, stood bravely erect on fissured spots here and there, telling storm and avalanche stories of hundreds of winters. The view of the lake from the top is, I think, the best of all. There is another rock, more striking in form than this, standing isolated at the lake's head, but it is not more than half as high. It is a knob of burnished granite, about a thousand feet high, apparently as flawless and strong in structure as a wave-worn pebble, and owes its existence to superior resistance offered to the overflowing ice-flood.

Made sketch of the lake, and sauntered back to camp, my iron-shod shoes clanking on the pavements, disturbing the chipmunks and birds. After dark went out to the shore—not a breath of air, the lake a perfect mirror reflecting sky and mountains with their stars and trees and wonderful sculpture, all their grandeur refined and doubled—a picture that seemed to belong more to heaven than earth.

August 9. I went ahead of the flock, and over the divide between the Merced and Tuolumne Basins. The gap between the east end of the Hoffman spur and the mass of mountain rocks about Cathedral Peak, though roughened by waving folds, seems to be one of the channels of a broad ancient glacier that came from the mountains on the summit of the range. In crossing this divide the ice-river made an ascent of about five hundred feet from the Tuolumne meadows. This entire region must have been overswept by ice.

From the top of the divide, and also from the big Tuolumne Meadows, the wonderful mountain called Cathedral Peak is in sight. From every point of view it shows marked individuality. It is a majestic temple of one stone, hewn from the living rock, and adorned with spires and pinnacles in regular cathedral style. The dwarf pines on the roof look like mosses. I hope some time to climb to it to say my prayers and hear the stone sermons.

The big Tuolumne Meadows are flowery lawns, lying along the south fork of the Tuolumne River at a height of about eighty-five hundred to nine thousand feet above the sea, partially separated by forests and bars of glaciated granite. Here the mountains seem to have been cleared away or set back, so that wide-open views may be had in every direction. The upper end of the series lies at the base of Mount Lyell, the lower below the east end of the Hoffman Range, so the length must be about ten or twelve miles. They vary in width from a quarter of a mile to perhaps three quarters, and a good many branch meadows put out along the banks of the tributary streams. This is the most spacious and delightful high pleasure ground I have yet seen. The air is bracing, yet warm during the day; and though high in the sky, the surrounding mountains are so much higher, one feels protected as if in a grand hall.

Mounts Dana and Gibbs, massive red mountains, perhaps thirteen thousand feet high or more, bound the view on the east, the Cathedral and Unicorn Peaks, with many nameless peaks, on the south, the Hoffman Range on the west, and a number of peaks unnamed, as far as I know, on the north. One of these last is much like the Cathedral. Most grass of the meadows is fine and silky, with exceedingly slender leaves, making a close sod, above which the minute purple flowers seem to float, while the sod is enriched with at least three species of gentian and at least as many of orthocarpus, potentilla, ivesia, solidago, pentstemon, with their gay colors—

purple, blue, yellow, and red—all of which I may know better soon. A central camp will probably be made in this region, from which I hope to make long excursions into the surrounding mountains.

On the return trip I met the flock about three miles east of Lake Tenaya. Here we camped for the night near a small lake lying on top of the divide in a clump of the two-leaved pine. We are now about nine thousand feet above the sea. Small lakes abound in all sorts of situations—on ridges, along mountain sides, and in piles of moraine boulders, most of them mere pools. Only in those canyons of the larger streams at the foot of declivities, where the down thrust of the glaciers was heaviest, do we find lakes of considerable size and depth. How grateful a task it would be to trace them all and study them! How pure their waters are, clear as crystal in polished stone basins! None of them, so far as I have seen, have fishes, I suppose on account of falls making them inaccessible. One would think their eggs might get into these lakes by chance; on ducks' feet, for example, or in their mouths, or in their crops, as some plant seeds are distributed. Nature has so many ways of doing such things. How did the frogs, found in all the bogs and pools and lakes, however high, manage to get up these mountains? Surely not by jumping. Such excursions through miles of dry brush and boulders would be very hard on frogs. Perhaps their stringy gelatinous spawn is occasionally entangled or glued on the feet of waterbirds. Anyhow, they are here and in hearty voice. I like their cheery tronk and crink. They take the place of songbirds at a pinch.

August 10. Another of those exhilarating days that make the blood dance and excite nerves that render one well-nigh immortal. Had another view of the broad ice-ploughed divide, and gazed again and again at the Sierra temple and the great red mountains east of the meadows.

We are camped near the Soda Springs on the north side of the river. A hard time we had getting the sheep across. They were driven into a horseshoe bend and fairly crowded off the bank. They seemed willing to die rather than risk getting wet, though they swim well enough when they have to. Why sheep should be so unreasonably afraid of water, I don't know, but they do fear it as soon as they are born and perhaps before. I once saw a lamb a few hours old approach a stream about two feet wide and an inch deep, after it had walked only about a hundred yards on its life journey. All the flock had crossed this inch-deep stream; the mother and her lamb being last. As soon as the flock was out of the way, the anxious mother crossed over and called the youngster. It walked cautiously to the brink, gazed at the water, bleated piteously, and refused to venture. The patient mother went back to it again and again. Like the pilgrim on Jordan's stormy bank it feared to launch away. At length, gathering its trembling legs for the effort, throwing up its head as if wanting to keep its nose above water, it made the tremendous leap, and landed in the middle of the inch-deep stream. Astonished that only its toes were wet, it gazed at the shining water a few seconds, and then sprang to the shore safe and dry. All kinds of wild sheep are mountain animals, and their descendants' dread of water is not easily accounted for.

August 11. Fine shining weather, with ten minutes of noon thunderstorm. Rambling all day getting acquainted with the region north of the river. Found a small lake and many charming glacier meadows embosomed in a forest of the two-leaved pine, growing on broad, almost continuous deposits of moraine material. It is remarkably in its growth, and the trees are much closer together than in any of the fir or pine woods farther down the range. The evenness of the growth would seem to indicate that the trees are nearly all of the same age – probably in great part the result of fire. I saw several large patches and strips of bleached spars, the ground beneath them covered with a young even growth. Fire can run in these wood because the tree bark is dripping with resin and the growth is close, and the soil produces crops of tall broad-leaved grasses on which fire can travel, even when the weather is calm. Besides these fire-killed patches there are many uprooted trees here and there, some with the bark and needles still on, as if they had lately been blown down in some thunderstorm blast. Saw a large black-tailed deer, a buck with antlers like the upturned roots of a fallen pine.

After a long ramble through the dense woods I emerged on a smooth meadow like a lake of light, about a mile and a half long, a quarter to half a mile wide, and bounded by tall, arrowy pines. The sod, like that of all the glacier meadows locally, is made of silky agrostis and calamagrostis chiefly; their panicles of purple flowers and purple stems seeming to float above the green leaf plush like a thin misty cloud, while the sod is brightened by several species of gentian, potentilla, ivesia, orthocarpus, and their corresponding bees and butterflies. All the glacier meadows are beautiful, but few are so perfect as this one. Compared with it the most carefully leveled, licked, snipped artificial lawns are coarse things. I should like to live here always. It is so calm and withdrawn while open to the universe, communing with everything good. To the north I discovered the camp of some Indian hunters. Their fire was still burning, but they had not yet returned from the chase.

From meadow to meadow, every one beautiful beyond telling, and from lake to lake through groves and belts of arrowy trees, I held my way northward toward Mount Conness, finding telling beauty everywhere, while the encompassing mountains were calling "Come." Hope I may climb them all.

August 12. The sky-scenery has changed little with the change in elevation. Clouds about .05. Glorious pearly cumuli tinted with purple of ineffable fineness of tone. Moved camp to the side of the glacier meadow mentioned above. To let sheep trample so divine a place seems barbarous. Fortunately they prefer the succulent broad-leaved triticum and other woodland grasses to the silky species of the meadows, and therefore seldom set foot on them.

The shepherd and the Don cannot agree about herding. Billy sets his dog Jack on the sheep far too often, so the Don thinks; and after some dispute, in which the shepherd loudly claimed the right to dog the sheep as he pleased, he started for the plains. Now the care of the sheep will fall on me, though Mr. Delaney promises to do the herding himself before returning to the lowlands for another shepherd, leaving me free to rove as I like.

Had another rich ramble. Pushed north beyond the forests to the head of the general basin, where traces of glacial action are strikingly clear. The recesses among the peaks look like quarries, so raw and fresh are the moraine chips and boulders that strew the ground in Nature's glacial workshops.

Soon after my return to camp we had a visit from an Indian, probably one of the hunters whose camp I had discovered. He came from Mono, he said, with others of his tribe, to hunt deer. One that he had killed nearby he was carrying on his back, its legs tied together in an ornamental bunch on his forehead. Throwing down his burden, he gazed stolidly for a few minutes in silent Indian fashion, then cut off eight or ten pounds of venison for us, and begged a "lill" (little) of everything he saw or could think of—flour, bread, sugar, tobacco, whiskey, needles, etc. We gave a fair price for the meat in flour and sugar and added a few needles.

A strangely dirty and irregular life these dark, half-happy savages lead in this clean wilderness—starvation and abundance, deathlike calm, indolence, and admirable, indefatigable action succeeding each other in stormy rhythm like winter and summer. Two things they have that civilized toilers might well envy them—pure air and pure water. These go far to cover and cure the grossness of their lives. Their food is mostly berries, pine nuts, clover, lily bulbs, wild sheep, antelope, deer, grouse, sage hens, and the larvæ of ants, wasps, bees, and other insects.

August 13. Day all sunshine, dawn and evening purple, noon gold, no clouds, air motionless. Mr. Delaney arrived with two shepherds, one was an Indian. On his way up he left some provisions at the Portuguese camp on Porcupine Creek near our old Yosemite camp, and I set out this morning to fetch them. Arrived at the Porcupine camp at noon, and might have returned to the Tuolumne late in the evening, but decided to stay overnight with the Portuguese shepherds at their pressing invitation. They had sad stories to tell of losses from the Yosemite bears, and were so discouraged they seemed on the point of leaving the mountains; for the bears came every night and helped themselves in spite of all their efforts to keep them off.

I spent the afternoon in a grand ramble along the Yosemite walls. From the highest the Three Brothers rocks, I saw all the upper half of the valley floor and nearly all the rocks walls on both sides and at the head, with snowy peaks in the background. Saw also the Vernal and Nevada Falls, a truly glorious picture—rocky permanence combined with evanescent plants frail and fine; water descending in thunder, then gliding through meadows and groves in gentlest beauty.

This standpoint is about eight thousand feet above the sea, or four thousand feet above the floor of the valley, and every tree, though looking small and feathery, stands in admirable clearness, and the shadows they cast are as distinct in outline as if seen at a distance of a few yards. They appeared even more so. No words will ever describe the charm of this mountain park—Nature's landscape garden at once tenderly beautiful and sublime. No wonder it draws nature lovers from all over the world.

Glacial action even on this lofty summit is plainly displayed. Not only has all the lovely valley now smiling in sunshine been filled to the brim with ice, but it has been deeply overflowed.

I visited our old Yosemite campground at the head of Indian Creek, and found it fairly smoothed down with bear-tracks. The bears had eaten all the sheep that were smothered in the corral, and some of the grand animals must have died, for Mr. Delaney had put a large quantity of poison in the carcasses. All sheep-men carry strychnine to kill coyotes, bears, and panthers, though neither coyotes nor panthers are numerous in the upper mountains. The little dog-like wolves are far more numerous in the foothills and plains, where they find more food—saw only one panther-track above eight thousand feet.

After sunset in the Portuguese camp I found the two shepherds greatly excited over the bears that have learned to like mutton. "They are getting worse and worse," they lamented. Not willing to wait decently until after dark, they come eat their fill in broad daylight.

The evening before my arrival, when the two were leisurely driving the flock toward camp half an hour before sunset, a hungry bear came out of the chaparral within a few yards, and shuffled deliberately toward the flock. "Portuguese Joe," who always carried a gun with buckshot, fired, threw down his gun, climbed the nearest suitable tree to a safe height without waiting to see the effect of his shot. His companion also ran, but said the bear rose on its hind legs and threw out its arms, then went into the brush as if wounded.

At another of their camps, a bear with two cubs attacked the flock before sunset, just as they were approaching the corral. Joe promptly climbed a tree, while Antone, rebuking his companion for cowardice, said that he was not going to let bears "eat up his sheeps," and rushed towards them, shouting and setting his dog on them. The frightened cubs climbed a tree, but the mother ran to meet the shepherd. Antone eyed the oncoming bear, then turned and fled, closely pursued. He ran to the camp and scrambled up to the roof of the little cabin; the bear followed, but did not climb the roof—only stood glaring up at him for a few minutes, threatening him, then went to her cubs, called them down, went to the flock, caught a sheep for supper, and vanished in the brush.

As soon as the bear left the cabin, the trembling Antone begged Joe to show him a good safe tree, up which he climbed like a sailor climbing a mast, and remained as long as he could hold on. After these disastrous experiences the shepherds gathered large piles of dry wood and made a ring of fire around the corral every night, while one with a gun kept watch from a comfortable stage built on a neighboring pine. This evening the show made by the circle of fire was very fine, bringing out the trees in most impressive relief, and making the thousands of sheep eyes glow like a glorious bed of diamonds.

August 14. When I went to bed last night all was quiet, though we expected the shaggy freebooters every minute. They did not come till near midnight, when a pair climbed in, killed two sheep and smothered ten, while the frightened watcher in the tree did not fire a single shot, saying that he was afraid he might kill some of the sheep, for the bears got into the corral before he got a good clear view of them. I told the shepherds they should move the flock to another camp. "Oh, no use, no use," they lamented; "where we go, the bears go too. See my poor dead sheeps—soon all dead. No use try another camp. We go down to the plains." And as I afterwards learned, they were driven out of the mountains a month before the usual time. Were bears much more numerous and destructive, the sheep would be kept away altogether.

It seems strange that bears, so fond of flesh, running the risks of guns, fires and poison, should never attack men except in defense of their young. How easily and safely a bear could pick us up as we lie asleep! Only wolves and tigers seem to have learned to hunt man for food, and perhaps sharks and crocodiles. Mosquitoes and other insects might devour a man in some parts of the world, and so might lions, leopards, wolves, hyenas, and panthers at times if pressed by hunger,—but under ordinary circumstances, perhaps, only the tiger may be said to be a man-eater—unless we add man himself.

Clouds as usual about .05. Another glorious Sierra day, fragrant, and clear. Many of the flowering plants have gone to seed, but many others are unfolding their petals every day, and the pines are more fragrant than ever. Their seeds are nearly ripe, and will soon be flying in the merriest flocks that ever spread a wing.

On the way back to our Tuolumne camp, I enjoyed the scenery if possible more than at first. Every feature already seems familiar as if I had lived here always. I never weary gazing at the wonderful Cathedral. It has more individual character than any other rock or mountain I ever saw, excepting perhaps the Yosemite South Dome. The forests, too, seem kindly familiar, and the lakes and meadows and glad singing streams. I should like to dwell with them forever. Here with bread and water I should be content. Even if not allowed to roam and climb, tethered to a tree in some meadow, even then I should be content forever. Watching the expressions ever varying on the faces of the mountains, watching the stars, which here have a glory that the lowlander never dreams of, watching the circling seasons, listening to the songs of the waters and winds and birds, would be endless pleasure.

And what glorious cloudlands I should see, storms and calms—a new heaven and a new earth [Biblical ref: Rev 21:1] every day, yes and new inhabitants. And how many visitors I should have. I feel sure I should not have one dull moment. And why should this appear extravagant? It is only common sense, a sign of health, all-awake health. One would be at an endless Godful play, and what speeches and music and acting and scenery and lights!—sun, moon, stars, auroras. Creation just beginning, the morning stars "still singing together and all the sons of God shouting for joy." [Biblical ref: Job 38:7].

August 21. Have just returned from a fine wild excursion across the range to Mono Lake, by way of the Bloody Canyon Pass. Mr. Delaney has been good to me, lending a helping hand at every opportunity, as if my wild notions and studies were his own. He is one of those remarkable California men who have been remodeled by the excitements of the gold fields, like the Sierra landscapes by grinding ice, bringing the harder ridges of character into relief—a tall, lean, big-hearted Irishman, educated for a priest in Maynooth College—lots of good, shining out now and then in this mountain light. Recognizing my love of wild places, he told me one evening that I ought to go through Bloody Canyon. He had not been there himself, he said, but had heard many of his mining friends speak of it as the wildest pass.

Of course I was glad to go. It lies just east of our camp and swoops down range's summit to the edge of the Mono Desert, descending four thousand feet in about four miles. It was traveled by animals and Indians long before its 'discovery' in the gold year of 1858. Many old trails come together at the head of it. The name may be from the red metamorphic slates, or by blood stains on the rocks?

Early in the morning I tied my notebook and some bread to my belt, and strode away feeling that I was going to have a glorious revel. The glacier meadows along my way soothed my morning speed, for the sod was full of blue gentians and daisies, kalmia and dwarf vaccinium, calling for recognition as old friends. As well, I had to stop to examine the rocks over which the ancient glacier had passed with tremendous pressure, polishing them so well they reflected sunlight like glass in some places, while fine striæ, seen through a lens, indicated the ice flow's direction.

On some of the pavements abrupt steps occur, showing that large masses of the rock had given way to the pressure, as well as small particles; moraines, too, scattered or like long curving embankments and dams, occur here and there, giving the region a new-made appearance. I watched the dwarfing of pines and nearly all the rest of the vegetation as I climbed. On Mammoth Mountain, to the south of the pass, I saw many gaps in the woods where avalanches had swept away every tree in their paths as well as the soil they were growing in, leaving bare bedrock. Only trees well anchored in clefts of the rock were broken off near the ground rather than uprooted.

It seems strange at first sight that trees that had been allowed to grow for a century or more should be thus swished away at a stroke. Such avalanches can only occur under rare conditions. No doubt on some positions of the mountain slopes the angle of the surface is such that avalanches must occur every winter. I noticed a few clean-swept slopes of this kind, where no vegetation can take root. The uprooted trees that had grown in the path of "century avalanches" were piled in windrows, and tucked snugly against the walling trees of the gaps, heads downward. A few were carried out into the open ground of the meadows, where the avalanches had stopped. Young pines, mostly the two-leaved and the white-barked, are already springing up in these cleared gaps. By ascertaining the age of these saplings, we should gain an approximation to the year the avalanches occurred. Perhaps most or all of them occurred in the same winter. How glad I should be to pursue such studies!

Near the summit at the head of the pass I found a species of dwarf willow flat on the ground, making a nice, soft, silky gray carpet, not a single stem or branch more than three inches high; but the catkins erect and making a close, nearly regular gray growth, being larger than all the rest of the plants. Some of these interesting dwarfs have only one catkin—willow bushes reduced to their lowest terms. I found patches of dwarf vaccinium also forming smooth carpets, and covered with round pink flowers in abundance, as if fallen from the sky like hail. A little higher, almost at the head of the pass, I found the blue arctic daisy and purple-flowered bryanthus, the mountain's own darlings, gentle mountaineers face to face with the sky, kept safe by a thousand miracles, seeming always the finer the wilder their homes. The trees, tough and resiny, seem unable to go a step farther; but far above the tree-line, these tender plants cheerily spread their gray and pink carpets right up to the very edges of the snow-banks in the hollows. Here, too, is the familiar robin, tripping on the flowery lawns, bravely singing the same cheery song I first heard when a boy in Wisconsin newly arrived from old Scotland.

In this fine company, I at length entered the gate of the pass, and the huge rocks began to close around me in all their mysterious impressiveness. Just then I was startled by a lot of hairy, muffled creatures coming shuffling, wallowing toward me as if they had no bones in their bodies. What a picture they made contrasted with the others I had just been admiring. They were only a band of Indians from Mono on their way to Yosemite for a load of acorns. They were wrapped in blankets made of the skins of sage-rabbits. The dirt on some of the faces seemed almost old enough and thick enough to have a geological significance; some were strangely blurred and divided into sections by wrinkles that looked like cleavage joints, and had a worn look as if they had lain exposed to the weather for ages.

I tried to pass them without stopping, but they wouldn't let me; forming a dismal circle about me, I was closely besieged while they begged whiskey or tobacco, and it was hard to convince them that I hadn't any. How glad I was to get away from the gray, grim crowd! Yet it seems sad to feel such desperate repulsion from one's fellow beings, however degraded. To prefer the society of squirrels and woodchucks to that of our own species must surely be unnatural. So with a fresh breeze and a hill between us I must wish them Godspeed and try to pray and sing with Burns, "It's coming yet, for a' that, that man to man, the world o'er, shall brothers be for a' that." ['for all that' – meaning despite all the bad blood that has passed between humans]

How the day went by I hardly know. By the map I have come only ten or twelve miles, though the sun is low in the west, showing I must have lingered, observing, sketching, taking notes among the glaciated rocks, moraines and Alpine flowerbeds.

At sundown the somber crags were inspired with the ineffable beauty of the alpenglow. A solemn stillness hushed everything. I crept into a hollow by a small lake near the head of the canyon, smoothed a sheltered spot, and gathered a few pine tassels for a bed. After the short twilight I kindled a fire, made a tin of tea, and lay down to watch the stars. Soon the night-wind began to flow from the snowy peaks overhead, gaining in strength, till in less than an hour it rumbled like a boisterous stream in a boulder-choked channel, moaning down the canyon as if bound on fateful work. Mingled with these stormy tones were those of the waterfalls on the canyon's north side, now sounding distinctly, now smothered by the heavier cataracts of air, making a glorious psalm of savage wildness.

My fire squirmed and struggled as if ill at ease, for though in a sheltered nook, detached masses of icy wind often fell like icebergs on top of it, scattering sparks and coals, so that I had to keep well back to avoid being burned. But the big resiny roots and knots of the dwarf pine could neither be beaten out nor blown away, and the flames, now rushing up in long lances, now flattened and twisted on the rocky ground, roared as if trying to tell the storm stories of the trees they belonged to, as the light given out was telling the story of the sunshine they had gathered in centuries of summers.

The stars shone clear in the strip of sky between the huge cliffs as I lay recalling the lessons of the day. Suddenly the full moon looked down over the canyon wall with a face of eager concern, which startled me, as if she had left her sky place and come to gaze on me alone, like a person entering one's bedroom. It was hard to realize that she was looking abroad on half the globe, lands and seas, mountains, plains, cities with their myriads of inhabitants sleeping and waking, sick and well. No, she seemed to be just on the rim of Bloody Canyon and looking only at me. This was indeed getting near to Nature.

I remember watching the harvest moon rising above the oaks in Wisconsin - apparently big as a cart-wheel and not half a mile distant. With these exceptions I might say I never before had seen the moon, and this night she seemed so near, the effect was marvelously impressive and made me forget the Indians, the black rocks above me and the uproar of the winds and waters making their way down the huge jagged gorge. I slept but little and gladly welcomed the dawn over the Mono Desert. By the time I had made a cup of tea, sunbeams were pouring through the canyon, and I set forth, gazing eagerly at the tremendous walls of red slates savagely and apparently ready to fall in avalanches fit to choke the pass and fill up the lakelets. I bounded lightly from rock to rock, admiring the polished bosses shining gloriously in the slant sunshine in the general roughness of moraines and avalanche taluses, even near the head of the canyon and the highest fountains of the ice.

Here, too, are most of the lowly plant people now opening their beautiful eyes. None could fail to glory in Nature's tender care for them in so wild a place. The little ouzel is flitting from rock to rock along Canyon Creek, diving for breakfast in icy pools, and merrily singing as if the huge, avalanche-swept gorge was the most delightful of all its mountain homes. Besides a high fall on the north wall, apparently coming direct from the sky, there are many narrow cascades, now contracted and out of sight, now leaping from ledge to ledge in filmy sheets through which the sunbeams sift. On the main Canyon Creek, to which all these are tributary, is a series of small falls and rapids down to the foot of the canyon, interrupted only by the lakes in which the waters rest.

One of the finest of the cascades is outspread on the face of a precipice, its waters separated into ribbon-like strips, and woven into a diamond-like pattern by tracing the cleavage joints of the rock, while tufts of bryanthus, grass, sedge, saxifrage form beautiful fringes. Who could imagine beauty so fine in so savage a place? Gardens are blooming in all sorts of nooks and hollows—at the head alpine eriogonums, erigerons, saxifrages, gentians, [long list of species].

One of the smallest cascades in the lower pass, which I name the Bower Cascade, is verged by snowy and luxuriant vegetation. Wild rose and dogwood form dense masses overarching the stream, and out of this bower the creek, grown strong with many in-dashing tributaries, leaps forth into the light, and descends in a fluted curve thick-sown with flashing spray. At the foot of the canyon there is a lake formed by the damming of the stream by a terminal moraine.

The three other lakes in the canyon are in basins eroded from solid rock, where the pressure of the glacier was greatest, and the most resisting portions of the basin rims are beautifully polished. Below Moraine Lake there are several old lake-basins lying between large lateral moraines which extend out into the desert. These basins are now filled up by stream-borne material, and changed to dry sandy flats covered mostly by grass and artemisia and sun-loving flowers. All of these lower lake-basins were evidently formed by terminal moraine dams deposited where the receding glacier had lingered during short periods of less waste, or greater snowfall, or both.

Looking up the canyon from the sunny edge of the Mono plain my morning ramble seems a dream, so great is the change in vegetation and climate. The lilies on the bank of Moraine Lake are higher than my head, and the sunshine is hot enough for palms. Yet the snow round the arctic gardens at the summit of the pass is plainly visible about four miles away, and in between lie specimen zones of all the principal climates of the globe. In little more than an hour one may go from winter to summer, from an Arctic to a torrid region, through as great changes of climate as one would traveling from Labrador to Florida.

The Indians I had met near the head of the canyon had camped at the foot of it the night before they made the ascent, and I found their fire still smoking on the side of a small tributary stream near Moraine Lake; and on the edge of what is called the Mono Desert, four or five miles from the lake, I came to a patch of elymus, or wild rye, growing in magnificent waving clumps six or eight feet high, bearing heads six to eight inches long. The crop was ripe, and Indian women were gathering the grain in baskets by bending down large handfuls, beating out the seed, and fanning it in the wind. The grains are about five eighths of an inch long, dark-colored and sweet. I fancy the bread made from it must be as good as wheat bread. A fine squirrelish employment this wild grain-gathering seems, and the women were evidently enjoying it, laughing and chattering and looking almost natural, though most Indians I have seen are not a whit more natural in their lives than we civilized whites.

Perhaps if I knew them better I should like them better. The worst thing about them is their uncleanliness. Nothing truly wild is unclean. Down on the shore of Mono Lake I saw a number of their flimsy huts on the banks of streams that dash into that dead sea— mere brush tents where they lie at their ease. Some of the men were feasting on buffalo berries, lying beneath the tall bushes now red with fruit. The berries are rather insipid, but they must needs be wholesome, since for days and weeks the Indians, it is said, eat nothing else. In the season they in like manner depend chiefly on the fat larvæ of a fly that breeds in the salt water of the lake, or on the big corrugated caterpillars of a silkworm that feeds on the yellow pine. Occasionally a grand rabbit-drive is organized and hundreds are slain with clubs on the lake shore, chased into a dense crowd by dogs, children, men and women, and rings of sage brush fire. The skins are made into blankets.

In autumn the better hunters bring in many deer, (and rarely a wild sheep) from the high peaks. Antelopes used to be abundant on the desert at the base of the ranges. Sage hens, grouse, and squirrels help vary their wild diet of worms; pine nuts also from the *Pinus monophylla*, and good bread and mush are made from acorns and wild rye.

Strange to say, they seem to like the lake larvæ best of all. Long windrows are washed up, which they gather and dry like grain for winter use. It is said that wars, on account of encroachments on each other's worm-grounds, are of common occurrence among the various tribes and families.

Each claims a certain marked portion of the shore. The pine nuts are delicious—large quantities are gathered every autumn. The tribes of the west flank of the range trade acorns for worms and pine nuts. The women backpack immense loads through the passes and down the range, making journeys of about forty or fifty miles each way.

The desert around the lake is surprisingly flowery.

Opposite the mouth of the canyon a range of volcanic cones extends southward from the lake, rising abruptly out of the desert like a chain of mountains, like heaps of loose ashes that have never been blest by either rain or snow, but, 'for all that,' yellow pines are climbing their gray slopes, trying to clothe them and give beauty for ashes [Biblical ref: Isaiah 61:3 for those who grieve in Zion, to bestow on them a crown of beauty instead of ashes, the oil of joy instead of mourning]. A country of contrasts: deserts bounded by snow-laden mountains—cinders and ashes scattered on glacier-polished pavements—frost and fire working together in the making of beauty. In the lake are several volcanic islands - the waters were once mingled with fire.

Glad to get back to the green side of the mountains.. Reading these grand mountain manuscripts: every vicissitude of heat and cold, calm and storm, upheaving volcanoes and down-grinding glaciers, we see that everything in Nature called destruction must also be a creation—a change from beauty to beauty.

Our glacier meadow camp north of Soda Springs seems more beautiful every day. The grass covers all the ground though the leaves are thread-like in fineness, and in walking it seems like a plush carpet of marvelous richness. It is richer in flowering plants than the prairies of Wisconsin and Illinois were in all their wild glory.

The showy flowers are mostly three gentian species, a purple and yellow orthocarpus, a golden-rod or two, a small blue pentstemon almost like a gentian, [list of other species]. Through this flowery lawn flows a silent stream about three feet wide in most places, widening here and there into pools six or eight feet in diameter with no apparent current, the banks bossily rounded. There are rugs of bryanthus spreading here and there over sunken boulders. Leaving the meadow, the stream sings merrily down over shelving rock ledges on its way to the Tuolumne River.

Meanwhile, the sublime, massive Mount Dana and its companions, green, red, and white, loom impressively above the pines along the eastern horizon.

CHAPTER X

THE TUOLUMNE CAMP

August 22. Clouds none, cool west wind, slight hoarfrost on the meadows. Carlo is missing; have been seeking him all day. In the thick woods among tall grass and fallen pines, I discovered a baby fawn. At first it seemed inclined to come to me; but when I tried to catch it it turned and walked softly away, choosing its steps like a cautious cat; suddenly it began to buck and run like a grown deer, jumping high. Possibly its mother may have called it, but I did not hear her.

Carlo, I am distressed! There are several other camps and dogs not many miles from here, and I still hope to find him. He never left me before. Panthers are very rare here, and I don't think any of these cats would dare touch him. He knows bears too well to be caught by them, and as for Indians, they don't want him.

August 23. Cool, bright day, hinting Indian summer. Carlo has come back. He was at a camp a few miles to the northwestward. He looked sheepish and ashamed when I asked him where he had been - now trying to get me to show signs of forgiveness. A wondrous wise dog. I could not have left the mountains without him.

Rose and crimson sunset, and soon after the stars appeared the moon rose in most impressive majesty over the top of Mount Dana. I sauntered up the meadow in the white light. The jet-black tree-shadows were substantial looking, I often stepped high in crossing them, taking them for charred logs.

August 24. Another charming day, warm and calm soon after sunrise, clouds only about .01,—faint, silky cirrus wisps, scarcely visible. Slight frost, Indian summerish, the mountains softer in outline and dreamy looking, their roughness melted off.

Sky at evening with fine, dark, subdued purple, almost like the evening purple of the San Joaquin plains.

August 25. Cool as usual in the morning, quickly changing to the ordinary serene warmth. Toward evening the west wind was cool and sent us to the camp-fire. Of all Nature's flowery carpeted mountain halls none can be finer than this glacier meadow. Bees and butterflies seem as abundant as ever. The birds are still here, showing no sign of leaving for winter quarters though the frost must bring them to mind. For my part I should like to stay here all winter or all my life or even all eternity.

August 26. Frost this morning; all the meadow grass and some of the pine needles sparkling with irised crystals—flowers of light. Large picturesque clouds, craggy like rocks, are piled on Mount Dana, reddish like the mountain itself; the sky for a few degrees around the horizon is pale purple, into which the pines dip their spires with fine effect. Spent the day as usual looking about me, watching the changing lights, the ripening autumn colors of the grass, seeds, late-blooming gentians, asters, goldenrods; parting the meadow grass and looking down into the underworld of mosses and liverworts; watching the busy ants and beetles and other small people at work and play like squirrels and bears in a forest; studying the formation of lakes and meadows, moraines, mountain sculpture; making small beginnings in these directions, charmed by the serene beauty of everything.

The day has been extra cloudy, though bright on the whole, for the clouds were brighter than usual. Clouds about .15, which in Switzerland would be considered extra clear. Probably more free sunshine falls on this majestic range than on any other in the world I've ever heard of. It has the brightest weather, brightest glacier-polished rocks, the greatest abundance of irised waterfall spray, the brightest silver firs and silver pines, more star-shine, moonshine, and perhaps more crystal-shine than any other mountain chain, and its countless mirror lakes, having more light poured into them, glow and spangle most. And how glorious the shining after the short summer showers and after frosty nights when the morning sunbeams are pouring through the crystals on the grass and pine needles, and how spiritually fine is the morning-glow on the mountain-tops and the alpenglow of evening. Well may the Sierra be named, not the Snowy Range, but the Range of Light.

August 27. Clouds few, mostly white and pink cumuli over the Hoffman spur towards evening—frosty morning. Crystals grow in marvelous beauty and perfection of form these still nights, every one built as carefully as the grandest holiest temple, as if planned to endure forever.

Contemplating the lace-like fabric of streams outspread over the mountains, we are reminded that everything is flowing—going somewhere, animals and so-called lifeless rocks as well as water. Thus the snow flows fast or slow, making glaciers and avalanches; the air in majestic floods carrying minerals, plant leaves, seeds, spores, with streams of music and fragrance; water streams carrying rocks both in solution and in the form of mud particles, sand, pebbles, and boulders. Rocks flow from volcanoes like water from springs, and animals flock and flow in currents modified by stepping, leaping, gliding, flying, swimming, etc. While the stars go streaming through space pulsed on and on forever like blood globules in Nature's warm heart. [Another paragraph of Muirish excesses – or is it simply poetic exuberance? What he says is both scientifically acute and poetically true].

August 28. The dawn a glorious song of color. Sky absolutely cloudless. A fine hoarfrost. Warm after ten o'clock. The gentians don't mind the first frost though their petals seem so delicate; they close every night as if going to sleep, and awake fresh as ever. The grass is a shade browner since last week, but there are no nipped wilted plants of any sort. Butterflies and the grand host of smaller flies are benumbed every night, but they dance in the sunbeams over the meadows before noon with no apparent lack of joyful life. Soon they must all fall like petals in an orchard, dry and wrinkled, not a wing of all the mighty host left to tingle the air. Nevertheless, new myriads will arise in the spring, rejoicing, exulting, as if laughing cold death to scorn.

August 29. Clouds about .05, slight frost. Bland serene Indian summer. Have been gazing all day at the mountains, watching the changing lights. More and more they clothed with light as a garment, white tinged with pale purple, palest during the midday hours, richest in the morning and evening. Everything seems consciously peaceful, thoughtful, waiting God's will.

August 30. This day just like yesterday. A few clouds motionless and apparently with no work beyond looking beautiful. Frost enough for crystal building—glorious fields of ice-diamonds destined to last but a night. How lavish is Nature creating, destroying, chasing every material particle from form to form, ever changing, ever beautiful!

Mr. Delaney arrived this morning. Felt not a trace of loneliness while he was gone. On the contrary, I never enjoyed grander company. The whole wilderness seems to be familiar, full of humanity. The very stones seem talkative, brotherly. No wonder when we consider that we all have the same Father and Mother.

August 31. Clouds .05. Silky cirrus wisps and fringes so fine they almost escape notice. Frost enough for another crop of crystals on the meadows but none on the forests. The gentians, goldenrods, asters, etc., don't seem to feel it; neither petals nor leaves are touched though they seem so tender. Every day opens and closes like a flower, noiseless, effortless. Divine peace glows on all the majestic landscape like the silent enthusiastic joy that sometimes transfigures a noble human face. [Greek: en-thousiasmos – filled with spirit].

Yosemite falls (painting by Robert Wilson)

September 1. Clouds .05 — motionless, of no particular color — ornaments with no hint of rain or snow. Day all calm — another grand throb of Nature's heart, ripening late flowers and seeds for next summer, full of life and plans of life to come, and full of ripe and ready death beautiful as life, telling divine wisdom and immortality. Have been up Mount Dana, to see as much as I can now that the time of departure is drawing nigh. The views from the summit reach eastward over the Mono Lake and Desert; mountains beyond mountains looking barren and bare like heaps of ashes dumped from the sky. The lake, eight or ten miles in diameter, shines like a burnished disk of silver, no trees about its gray, ashy, cindery shores.

Looking westward, the glorious forests sweep over countless ridges and hills, girdling domes and mountains, fringing in long curving lines the dividing ridges, and filling every hollow where the glaciers have spread soil-beds, however rocky or smooth.

Looking north and south along the axis of the range, you see the glorious array of crags and peaks and snow, the fountain-heads of rivers that are flowing west to the sea through the famous Golden Gate, and east to hot salt lakes and deserts to evaporate and hurry back into the sky. Innumerable lakes are shining like eyes beneath heavy rock brows, bare or tree fringed, or embedded in black forests. Meadow openings in the woods seem as numerous as the lakes, or perhaps more so.

Far up the moraine-covered slopes and among crumbling rocks I found many hardy plants, some of them still in flower. The best gains of this trip were the lessons of unity and interrelation of all the features of the landscape revealed in general views.

Both lakes and meadows are located where the glaciers bore heaviest at the foot of the steepest parts of their channels, and of course their longest diameters are approximately parallel with each other and with forest belts in long curving lines on the lateral and medial moraines, and also in broad outspreading fields on the terminal beds, deposited when the glaciers were receding. The domes, ridges, and spurs also show the influence of glacial action in their forms; they are the forms of greatest resistance to the stress of over-sweeping, ice-streams; survivals of the most resisting masses, or those most favorably situated. [A sort of natural selection of rock forms under the stress of their predator – glaciers!]

Every rock, mountain, stream, plant, lake, lawn, forest, garden, bird, beast, insect seems to invite us to come and learn something of its history and relationship. But shall the poor ignorant scholar be allowed to try the lessons they offer? It seems too great and good to be true. Soon I'll be going to the lowlands. The bread camp must soon be removed. If I had a few sacks of flour, an axe, and some matches, I would build a cabin of pine logs, pile up plenty of firewood about it and stay all winter to see the grand fertile snow-storms, watch the birds and animals: how they live so high, how the forests look snow-laden or buried, how the avalanches look and sound on their way down the mountains. But for now I'll have to go, for there is nothing to spare in the way of provisions. I'll surely be back, however, surely I'll be back. No other place has ever so overwhelmingly attracted me as this hospitable, Godful wilderness.

September 2. A grand, red, rosy day—a perfection of a day. What it means I don't know. It is a noticeable change from tranquil sunshine, purple mornings and evenings and still, white noons. There is nothing like a storm, however. The average cloudiness only about

.08, [that is: eight per cent cloud cover] and there is no sighing in the woods to indicate a big change. The sky was red in the morning and evening, the color not the ordinary diffuse purple glow, but loaded upon separated motionless clouds anchored around the mountain-fenced horizon. A deep red cap lingered a long time on Mount Dana and Mount Gibbs, even hiding most of their bases, but leaving Dana's round summit free, which seemed to float separate and alone.

Mammoth Mountain, to the south of Gibbs and Bloody Canyon, striped with snow-banks and clumps of dwarf pine, was also favored with a generous crimson cap - a huge pile colored with a perfect crimson passion - important enough to be sent off to burn among the stars in majestic independence. One is constantly reminded of the infinite lavish fertility of Nature—inexhaustible abundance amid what seems enormous waste. And yet when we look into any of her operations, we learn that no particle of her material is wasted or worn out. It is eternally flowing from use to use, beauty to yet higher beauty: we soon cease to lament death, and rather to exult in the endless wealth of the universe, and faithfully wait the reappearance of everything that fades and dies, feeling sure that its next appearance will be better and more beautiful than the last. [However, as we now know, despite life's cycles, Nature is not inexhaustible at all, and we carry the sole responsibility for much of the destruction visible in the last few centuries].

Eagerly I watched the growth of these redlands of the sky as though new mountain ranges were being built. Soon the group of snowy peaks in which lie the sources of the Tuolumne, Merced, and North Fork of the San Joaquin were decorated with majestic colored clouds, their degree of complication reflecting the grand fountain-heads of the rivers they overshadowed. The Sierra Cathedral, to the south of camp, was overshadowed like Sinai [Biblical ref: Exodus 24:16 'And the glory of the Lord settled on Mount Sinai. For six days the cloud covered the mountain, and on the seventh day the Lord called to Moses from within the cloud].

Never before noticed so fine a union of rock and cloud, form and colour drawing earth and sky together as one; and so human is it, every feature and tint goes to one's heart, and we shout, exulting in wild enthusiasm as if all the divine show were our own. Here, more and more, we feel ourselves part of wild Nature and kin to everything. Spent most of the day high on the valley's north rim, commanding views of the clouds in all their red glory, while the rocks and trees and small Alpine plants at my feet seemed thoughtful, as if conscious spectators of this glorious cloud-world.

As I plodded higher I came to small garden-patches and ferneries where one would expect that no plant could possibly live. But, as in the region about the head of Mono Pass and the top of Dana, it was in the wildest, highest places that the most beautiful and tender and enthusiastic plant-people were found. Repeatedly I asked, How came you here? How do you live through the winter? Our roots, they explained, reach far down the joints of the summer-warmed rocks; beneath our snow mantle killing frosts cannot reach us while we sleep away the dark half of the year dreaming of spring.

Ever since I was allowed entrance here I have been looking for Cassiope, said to be the most beautiful and best-loved of the heathworts, but, strange to say, I have not yet found it. On my high mountain walks I keep muttering, "Cassiope, cassiope." This name, as Calvinists say, is driven in upon me, notwithstanding the glorious host of plants that come about me uncalled as soon as I show myself. Cassiope seems the highest name of all the small mountain-heath people, and as if conscious of her worth, keeps out of my way. I must find her soon, if at all this year.

[Plants with beautiful bell-like flowers, named after Cassiopeia in Greek mythology, whose boast of her and her daughter Andromeda's beauty drew the wrath of Poseidon, and ended in Andromeda tied to a post on the seashore awaiting the sea monster Cetus, and Cassiopeia herself being tied to a throne for eternity. There is a star constellation showing this last event]

September 4. All the vast sky dome is clear, filled only with mellow Indian summer light. The pine and hemlock and fir cones are nearly ripe and are falling fast all day, cut off and gathered by the busy squirrels. Almost all the plants have matured seeds, their summer work done; and the summer crop of birds and deer will soon follow their parents to the plains when the snow begins to fly.

September 5. Weather cool, cloudless, calm, bright as if no great thing was ready to be done. Have been sketching the North Tuolumne Church. The sunset gloriously colored.

September 6. Another perfectly cloudless day, purple evening and morning, all the middle hours one mass of serene sunshine. Soon after sunrise the air grew warm, and there was no wind. One naturally halted to see what Nature would do. There is a suggestion of real Indian summer in the hushed, faintly hazy weather. The thin yellow atmosphere is still plainly of the same general character as that of eastern Indian summer. The peculiar mellowness is perhaps in part caused by myriads of spores adrift in the sky.

Mr. Delaney now keeps up a solemn talk about the need of getting away from the mountains, telling sad stories of flocks that perished in storms that broke suddenly into the midst of fine innocent weather. "In no case," said he, "will I venture to stay so high and far back in the mountains as we now are later than the middle of this month, no matter how warm and sunny it may be." He would move the flock slowly at first, a few miles a day until the Yosemite Creek basin was reached and crossed, then while lingering in the heavy pine woods should the weather threaten he could hurry down to the foothills, where the snow never falls deep enough to smother a sheep.

Of course I want to see as much wilderness as possible in the few days left, and I say again—may the good time come when I can stay as long as I like with plenty of bread, far from trampling flocks, though I am thankful for this generous foodful inspiring summer. Anyhow we never know what guides we are to get—men, storms, guardian angels, or sheep. Perhaps everybody in the least natural is guarded more than he is aware. All the wilderness seems full of tricks to drive and draw us up into God's Light.

Have been busy planning, and baking bread for at least one more wild excursion among the high peaks, and surely none, however hopefully aiming at fortune or fame, ever felt so gloriously excited by the outlook.

September 7. Left camp at daybreak and made for Cathedral Peak, then struck east and south from that point at the heads of the Tuolumne, Merced, and San Joaquin Rivers. Down through the woods I went, across the Tuolumne River and meadows, and up the timbered slope bounding the upper Tuolumne basin to the south; thence along the east side of Cathedral Peak to its topmost spire, which I reached at noon, having loitered by the way to study the fine trees—two-leaved pine, mountain pine, albicaulis pine, silver fir, and the most charming, most graceful of all the evergreens, the mountain hemlock. High, cool, late-flowering meadows also detained me, and lakelets and avalanche tracks and huge quarries of moraine rocks above the forests.

All the way up from the Big Meadows to the base of the Cathedral the ground is covered with moraine, the left lateral moraine of the glacier that must have completely filled this upper Tuolumne basin. Higher there are several small terminal moraines of residual glaciers shoved forward at right angles against the grand simple lateral of the main Tuolumne Glacier. A fine place to study mountain sculpture and soil-making.

The view from the Cathedral Spires is very fine and telling in every direction. Innumerable peaks, ridges, domes, meadows, lakes, and woods; the forests extending in long curving lines and broad fields wherever the glaciers have left soil for them to grow, while the sides of the highest mountains show a straggling dwarf growth clinging to rock rifts apparently independent of soil. The dark heath-like growth on the Cathedral roof I found to be dwarf snow-pressed albicaulis pine, only three or four feet high, but very old looking. Many of them bear cones, and the noisy Clarke crow is eating the seeds, using his long bill like a woodpecker in digging them out.

Many flowers still about the peak's base, even on the roof among the little pines, especially a woody yellow-flowered eriogonum and a handsome aster. The Cathedral's body is nearly square, the upper slopes wonderfully symmetric, the ridge trending northeast and southwest, a direction apparently determined by structure joints in the granite. The gable on the northeast end is magnificently simple; at its base a big snow-bank is protected by shadow. The front is adorned with many pinnacles and a tall spire of curious workmanship. Here too the rock joints in the rock have played an important part in determining forms and size. The Cathedral is about eleven thousand feet above the sea, but the height is about fifteen hundred feet above the ridge it stands on. A mile or so west there is a handsome lake, and surrounding glacier-polished granite shines so bright it is hard to tell between rock and water. From up here I have a great view of this lake with its silvery basin and bits of meadow and groves; also of Lake Tenaya, Cloud's Rest and the South Dome of Yosemite, Mount Starr King, Mount Hoffman, the Merced peaks, and the vast multitude of snowy fountain peaks extending north and south along the axis of the range.

Of all the noble landscape, none seems more wonderful than the Cathedral itself, a temple displaying Nature's best masonry and sermons in stone. How often I have gazed at it from hills and ridges, and through forest openings on my many short excursions, devoutly wondering, admiring, longing!

This I may say is the first time I have been at church in California, every door graciously opened for the poor lonely worshiper. In our best times everything turns into religion, all the world seems a church and the mountains altars. And lo, here in front of the Cathedral is blessed Cassiope [a flower species], ringing her thousands of sweet bells, the sweetest church music I ever enjoyed. Listening, admiring, until late in the afternoon I compelled myself to hasten away east behind rough, splintery peaks, all of them granite like the Cathedral, sparkling with crystals—feldspar, quartz, hornblende, etc. Had a rather difficult creep across an immense snow and ice cliff, which gradually got steeper till it was almost impassable. Slipped on a dangerous place, but dug my heels into the thawing surface, stopping on the brink of a yawning ice gulf.

Camped beside a little pool and a group of dwarf pines; as I sit by the fire writing, the shallow pool seems fathomless with the infinite starry heavens in it, while the onlooking rocks and trees, tiny shrubs and daisies, brought forward in the glow, seem full of thought as if about to tell all their wild stories. An impressive meeting in which every one has something worthwhile to tell. And out in the solemn darkness beyond the fire-beams, how impressive is the music of a choir of rills singing their way down from snow to river! When we call to mind that thousands of these rejoicing rills are assembled in each one of the main streams, we wonder less that our Sierra rivers are songful all the way to the sea.

About sundown saw a flock of grayish sparrows going to roost in crevices of a crag above the big snow-field. Charming little mountaineers! Found a species of sedge in flower near a snow-bank. It can hardly have been out in the sun for more than a week, and is likely to be buried again in fresh snow in a month or so, thus making a winter about ten months long, while other seasons are perforce crowded into two months. How delightful it is to be alone here! How wild as the sky everything is and as pure! I shall never forget this big, divine day—the Cathedral and its myriad cassiope bells, the landscapes, and this camp in the crags, with its stars and streams and snow.

September 8. Day of scrambling, sliding on the peaks around the highest source of the Tuolumne and Merced. Climbed three of the most commanding mountains, whose names I don't know; crossed streams and huge beds of ice and snow more than I could keep count of. Neither could I keep count of the lakes scattered on tablelands and in the cirques of the peaks, and in chains in the canyons, linked by streams—a tremendously gray wilderness of shattered crags, ridges, and peaks, a few clouds drifting over and through the midst of them as if looking for work. In general, views of all the immense round landscape seem lifeless as a quarry, yet the most charming flowers were found rejoicing in countless nooks and garden-like patches everywhere. I must have done three or four days' climbing work in this one. Limbs perfectly tireless until near sundown, when I descended into the main upper Tuolumne valley at the foot of Mount Lyell, the camp still eight or ten miles distant. Going up through the pine woods past the Soda Springs Dome in the dark, where there is much fallen timber, and when the excitement of seeing things was lacking, I was tired. Arrived at the main camp at nine o'clock, and was soon sleeping sound as death.

CHAPTER XI

BACK TO THE LOWLANDS

September 9, 1869. Weariness eased, I feel eager for another excursion a month or two long in the same wonderful wilderness. Now, however, I must turn toward the lowlands, praying Heaven will shove me back again.

The most telling thing learned in these mountain excursions is the influence of cleavage joints on the features sculptured from the general mass of the range. Evidently the denudation has been enormous, while the inevitable outcome is subtle, balanced beauty. In general views, the features of the wildest landscape seem to be as harmoniously related as the features of a human face: they radiate spiritual beauty, divine thought, however covered and concealed by rock and snow.

Mr. Delaney has hardly had time to ask me how I enjoyed my trip, though he has facilitated my plans all summer, and declares I'll be famous some day, a kind guess that seems incredible to a wandering wilderness-lover with never a thought of fame while humbly trying to trace and enjoy Nature's lessons.

The camp stuff is now packed on the horses, and the flock is headed for the home ranch. Away we go, down through the pines, leaving the lovely lawn where we have camped so long. I wonder if I'll ever see it again. The sod is so tough and close it is scarce at all injured by the sheep. Fortunately they are not fond of silky glacier meadow grass. The day is perfectly clear, not a cloud or the faintest hint of a cloud is visible, and there is no wind. I wonder if in all the world, at a height of nine thousand feet, bright weather so steadily, faithfully calm may be found. We are going away fearing destructive storms, though it is difficult to conceive weather changes so great.

Though the water is now low in the river, the usual difficulty occurred in getting the flock across. Every one seemed invincibly determined to die any sort of dry death rather than wet its feet. Carlo has learned the sheep business like the best shepherd, and it is interesting to watch his intelligent efforts to push or frighten the silly creatures into the water. They had to be fairly crowded and shoved over the bank; and when at last one crossed because it could not get back, the whole flock suddenly plunged in headlong, as if the river was the only desirable part of the world. Aside from mere profit, one would rather herd wolves than sheep. As soon as they clambered up the opposite bank, they began baaing and feeding as if nothing unusual had happened. We crossed the meadows and drove slowly up the south rim of the valley through the same woods I had passed on my way to Cathedral Peak, and camped for the night by the side of a small pond on top of the big lateral moraine.

September 10. In the morning at daybreak not one of the two thousand sheep was in sight. Examining the tracks, we discovered that they had been scattered, perhaps by a bear. In a few hours all were found and gathered into one flock again. Had fine view of a deer. How graceful and perfect in every way it seemed as compared with the dusty, tousled sheep! From the high ground hereabouts had another grand view to the north—a heaving, swelling sea of domes and round-backed ridges fringed with pines, and bounded by innumerable sharp-pointed peaks, gray and barren-looking, though so full of beautiful life. Another day of the calm, cloudless kind, purple in the morning and evening. The evening glow has been very marked for the last two or three weeks. Perhaps the "zodiacal light."

September 11. Cloudless. Slight frost. Calm. Started fairly downhill, and now are camped at the west end meadows of Lake Tenaya—a charming place. Lake smooth as glass, mirroring its miles of glacier-polished pavements and bold mountain walls. Find aster still in flower. Here is about the upper limit of the dwarf form of the goldcup oak—eight thousand feet—about two thousand feet higher than the California black oak (*Quercus Californica*). Lovely evening, the reflections after dark marvelously impressive.

September 12. Cloudless day, all pure sun-gold. Among the magnificent silver firs once more, within two miles of the brink of Yosemite, at the famous Portuguese bear camp. Chaparral of goldcup oak, manzanita, and ceanothus abundant hereabouts, not present about the Tuolumne meadows, which is only little higher. The two-leaved pine, though far more abundant about the Tuolumne meadow region, reaches its greatest size on stream banks hereabouts and around boggy meadows. All the best dry ground is taken by the magnificent silver fir, which here reaches its greatest size and forms a well-defined belt. A glorious tree. Have fine bed of its boughs to-night.

September 13. Camp this evening at Yosemite Creek on a little sand flat near our old camp-ground. The vegetation is already yellow and dry; the creek almost dry. The slender form of the two-leaved pine on its banks is the handsomest I have seen anywhere. It might easily pass at first sight for a distinct species, though surely only a variety (*Murrayana*), due to rapid growth on good soil.

The yellow pine is as variable, or perhaps more so. The form here and a thousand feet higher, on crumbling rocks, is broad branching, with closely furrowed, reddish bark, large cones, and long leaves. It is one of the hardiest and most vital of pines, the tassels of long, stout needles silvery in the sun. When the wind is blows them all in the same direction, is one of the most splendid spectacles in the Sierra forests. This variety of *Pinus ponderosa* is regarded as a distinct species, *Pinus Jeffreyi*, by some botanists. The basin of this famous Yosemite stream is extremely rocky - like a street with big cobblestones. I wonder if I shall ever be allowed to explore it. It draws me so strongly, I would make any sacrifice to try to read its lessons. I thank God for this glimpse of it. The charms of these mountains are beyond all common reason, unexplainable and mysterious as life itself.

September 14. Nearly all day in magnificent fir forest, the top branches laden with erect gray cones shining with beads of balsam. The squirrels are cutting them off at a great rate. Bump, bump, I hear them falling, to be stored for winter bread. Those left by the industrious harvesters drop the scales and bracts when ripe, and it is fine to see the purple-winged seeds flying in merry-looking swirls to seek their fortunes. The bole and dead limbs of nearly every tree in the main forest-belt are ornamented by conspicuous tufts of a yellow lichen.

Camped for the night at Cascade Creek, near the Mono Trail crossing. Manzanita berries now ripe. Cloudiness today about .10 [meaing one tenth of the sky is clouded]. The sunset very rich, flaming purple and crimson showing gloriously through the aisles of the woods.

September 15. The weather pure gold, cloudiness about .05, white cirrus flecks and pencilings around the horizon. Move two or three miles and camp at Tamarack Flat. Wandering in the woods here back of the pines which bound the meadows, I found very noble specimens of the magnificent silver fir, the tallest about two hundred and forty feet high and five feet in diameter near the ground.

September 16. Crawled slowly four or five miles today through the glorious forest to Crane Flat, where we are camped for the night. The forests we so admired in summer seem still more beautiful and sublime in this mellow autumn light. Lovely starry night, the tall, spiring tree-tops relieved in jet black against the sky. I linger by the fire, loath to go to bed.

September 17. Left camp early. Ran over the Tuolumne divide and down a few miles to a grove of sequoias that I had heard of, directed by the Don. They occupy an area of less than a hundred acres. Some of the trees are noble, colossal old giants, surrounded by magnificent sugar pines and Douglas spruces. The perfect specimens not burned or broken are singularly regular, though not at all conventional, showing infinite and harmonious variety; the noble shafts with rich purplish-brown fluted bark, free of limbs for one hundred and fifty feet or so, ornamented here and there with leafy rosettes; main branches of the oldest trees very large, crooked and rugged, zigzagging stiffly outward seemingly lawless, yet stooping at the right distance from the trunk and dissolving in dense masses of branchlets, thus making a regular though greatly varied outline, the

king of all conifers, not only in size but in sublime majesty of
behavior and comportment.

I found a black, charred stump about thirty feet in diameter and
eighty or ninety feet high—a venerable monument of a tree that in
its prime may have been the monarch of the grove; seedlings and
saplings growing up here and there, thrifty and hopeful. Not any
unfavorable change of climate, but only fire, threatens the existence
of these noblest of God's trees. [Here Muir is wrong, for climate
change appears to be threatening the sequoia's existence, including
this famous grove]. Sorry I was not able to get a count of the old
monument's annual rings.

Camp this evening at Hazel Green, on the broad back of the dividing
ridge near our old camp-ground when we were on the way up in
spring. This ridge has the finest sugar-pine groves and finest
manzanita and ceanothus thickets I have yet found on all this
wonderful summer journey.

September 18. Made a long descent on the south side of the divide to
Brown's Flat, the grand forests left above us, though the sugar pine
still flourishes fairly well, and with the yellow pine, libocedrus, and
Douglas spruce, makes forests that would be considered most
wonderful in any other part of the world.

The Indians here, with great concern, pointed to an old garden patch
on the flat and told us to keep away from it. Perhaps some of their
tribe are buried here.

September 19. Camped this evening at Smith's Mill, on the first broad mountain bench reached in ascending the range, where pines grow large enough for good lumber. Here wheat, apples, peaches, and grapes grow, and we were treated to wine and apples. The wine I didn't like, but Mr. Delaney and the Indian driver and the shepherd seemed to think the stuff divine. Compared to sparkling Sierra water fresh from the heavens, it seemed a muddy, stupid drink. But the apples, best of fruits, how delicious they were—fit for gods or men.

On the way down from Brown's Flat we stopped at Bower Cave, and I spent an hour in it—one of the most novel and interesting of all Nature's underground mansions. Plenty of sunlight pours into it through the leaves of the four maple trees growing in its mouth, illuminating its clear, calm pool and marble chambers. A charming place, ravishingly beautiful, but the accessible parts of the walls are sadly disfigured with names of vandals.

September 20. The weather still golden and calm, but hot. We are now in the foothills, and all the conifers are left behind except the gray Sabine pine. Camped at the Dutch Boy's Ranch, where there are extensive barley fields showing nothing but dusty stubble.

September 21. A terribly hot, dusty, sunburned day.. reached the home ranch on the yellow San Joaquin plain.

September 22. The sheep were let out of the corral one by one, this morning, and counted. The losses are: ten killed by bears, one by a rattlesnake, one that had to be killed after a broken leg, and one that ran away on getting separated from the flock—thirteen all told. Of the other twelve doomed never to return, three were sold to ranchmen and nine were made into mutton.

Here ends my memorable first High Sierra excursion. I have crossed the Range of Light, surely the brightest and best of all the Lord has built; and rejoicing in its glory, I gratefully, hopefully pray I may see it again.

THE END

Afterword.

Surely few of us have had the same ecstatic response to landscape that John Muir had in his first summer in the Sierra. But then, who of us has suddenly been presented with what is arguably the best and grandest set of landscapes in the world? In his time, he was unlikely to have seen images of the Sierra before he got there – no search engines then with thousands of lovely photographs, no television laden with full color nature programs! Considering also his strict childhood in Scotland, his hard-labouring youth in Wisconsin and beyond, and the stern, overarching frown of Protestantism that shadowed his life - and we may begin to understand his utter delight and sense of freedom during his sheep-herding summer.

But that same landscape is now under serious threat. Humans have spent at least the last two hundred years pumping vast amounts of carbon dioxide into the air by the burning (mainly) of fossil fuels. This gas acts as a blanket, trapping the sun's radiance beneath it and causing global warming. Even in Muir's day the glaciers were beginning their retreat. This general retreat of ice and snow has accelerated in the last few years, confirming a general trend. The Sierra are a showcase of climate change – recently the snow pack has declined to around ten percent of last centuries' norms – the results are potentially catastrophic for the trees and rivers and everything else – nature being so densely inter-connected. On the other great masses of moist air coming east off the heated Pacific are causing huge sporadic floods in the area. To improve this situation takes an acknowledgment, a cooperation, a concerted set of actions that is perceived to erode employment and cost money – at least in the short term, though evidence is mounting that such actions supply more jobs and money than they take away. To say nothing of creating a better world.

Far-sighted modern economies in western Europe and giant economies in Asia are leading the effort against climate change. It is a pity that the USA – at least at federal level – seems content to be in the rear. The most dramatically beautiful landscapes in the world – the high Sierra – are the price to pay for this recalcitrance.

Muir's observations led him to see that everything is mutually dependent, including clouds and rocks. Humans are not exempt from this, though with our thirst for technological change we have arrogantly assumed we can craft our way free of Nature's demands and redress any mistake we have made. Not so. The cost of ignoring our mistakes is not only great to the natural world but to human society. We have no alternate home.

For these two reasons, Muir's example - that any human can passionately identify with Nature - and the modern threat to Nature of climate change, I would thus encourage readers to both get back to nature, wherever you are (lucky those people that can take to the

Sierra), and to work in their own lives for preservation of this natural wonderland - and in a wider sense, the planet itself.

NOTE ABOUT THE EDITOR.

Laurence de B Anderson was born in Africa and schooled there and in the US. He comes from a family of environmentalists (his grandfather helped establish the World Wildlife Fund, and his uncle AM Harthoorn helped invent the capture gun in Kenya, and was the inspiration for the TV program Daktari).

Growing up in Africa, he was surrounded by nature. In 1976 his family came to the US and spent three months in Alaska in the summer, as well as traversing many of the western states and the Pacific coast by sea and land, including the Inside Passage, the Yukon and Canada. It was an experience he never forgot. His first degree (in South Africa) was a BS in environmental and cell biology. Then he took fourth year Honours in Community Ecology, Evolution and Marine biology at the University of Auckland, New Zealand. A Masters in Cytogenetics/Zoology followed. He then became an artist and writer for several years, before taking an MD in order to become a physician.

But his commitment to the arts never wavered – he has continued to write books, make films and exhibit paintings for several decades. The life of John Muir has been a constant inspiration to him, and he has dedicated himself to re-presenting the great man's work to a 21st century public.

(Images in this publication are stock images, unless acknowledged otherwise. Having been selected for their subject matter: general natural beauty, some of them may not depict the Sierra area).

Frontispiece image by the author.